Copyight © 2025 by Taliesin Larmour-Jones & Phantom Writing

All rights reserved.

No portion of this book may be reproduced in any form without permission from the publisher or author, except as permitted by U.K. Copyright law.

Illustrations by Brian Jones
www.artofbrianjones.com/workinprogress/

With special thanks to Fiona Lintern, Lecturer in Psychology, for her guidance and feedback.

To Lorna, for her help and support with formatting and being a good friend.

To my family and friends who helped me improve this book, every step of the way. Thank you.

To you reading this, for thinking about your own wellbeing, instead of everyone else's and for taking the time to enjoy this book and learn something from it.

The Exchange Rate of Happiness

Chapter 1
What Are My Reasons for Writing This Book?........................... 6

Chapter 2
The Iceberg 12

Chapter 3
Ikigai: What Does Happiness Look Like To You? 24

Chapter 4
Finding Your Passion Through Doing 33

Chapter 5
Minding Your Mental 39

Chapter 6
Accepting Your Flaws and Setting Boundaries 51

Chapter 7
Strengthening Your Mental Walls:
Resilience and Perspective 59

Chapter 8
Creative Outlets & Reflection 69

Chapter 9
Goal Setting & Positive Habits 78

Chapter 10
Escaping Your Comfort Zone & Expanding Horizons 89

Chapter 11
Happiness As A Currency 95

Chapter 12
Putting the Brakes on Expectations 105

Chapter 13
Side-Hustling Your way Forward 114

Chapter 14
Surrounding Yourself with Like-Minded People 122

Chapter 15
Kill Your Ego 126

Chapter 16
Growing As a Person 134

Chapter 17
Creating for Others 139

Chapter 18
Closing Thoughts and Continued Practice 144

Chapter 1

What Are My Reasons for Writing This Book?

First off, I'd like to say thank you. Thank you for considering your own wellbeing and happiness.

In the busy hustle and bustle of life is it not always easy to remember to prioritise yourself, so well done. You have already taken the first step necessary to becoming happier; thinking about your own version of it. When you think about something or talk about it, you start to change it, even if just a little. It is how all ideas begin and actions start, the first step for any journey.

Now, I think it's time to tell you a little about myself and who I am, am I qualified to talk about happiness and what experiences have I got. Whilst we don't all have to be experts to write a worthwhile read, we do have to have interest, understanding or experience about the topic to write anything half-decent. Psychology fascinates me, humans are complex and we are all so different, this is one of the reasons I am pursuing a master's degree in the subject, on top of my own lived experiences and research within the field.

I have had my fair share of ups-and-downs, from struggling with mental health since I was a child to having two major depressive episodes, one nine years ago and the other six; unable to get out of bed with what felt like the energy levels of a zombie. Within that mix I also experienced an emotionally abusive relationship, splitting up with my fiancé, feeling like the weight of the world was on my shoulders, not having a job and being at my lowest point in life so far.

Since then I have come a long way and learned a lot about myself. How to manage and cope with poor mental health, how to open up and talk to others about how I am feeling, and employing coping mechanisms and strategies to build a happier life for myself. More recently I became medicated for work-related stress, depression and anxiety; as well as experiencing a couple of sessions of cognitive behavioural therapy (CBT). Suffice to say I am open-minded and understand how it can feel to suffer with poor mental health and to be unhappy. Thankfully, I am no longer medicated for stress and have learned how to set much healthier boundaries and manage a better work-life balance. I'll share with you some of the methods I have used to get to where I am now and the process of growing and becoming more resilient throughout this journey.

Through a lot of trial-and-error, coping strategies and positive habits I have started to build a much more fulfilling life. One where I am able to manage stresses and my mental health much better, whilst also doing the things I enjoy. I've had some helpful conversations with others struggling and the advice I have given has helped them to take the first steps toward becoming happier and building healthier habits into their life. I made the decision to start writing this book as I realised there must be others out there who could benefit from some of my own experiences and how to navigate through the emotional and psychological minefield we call life. I made that decision about four years ago, since then I have delved into the world of self-development, undertaken courses, read books and studied topics such as self-improvement, resilience, and mental health.

This book is something I have worked on-and-off for a few of years, putting it down and picking it back up again. You see, I'm terrible at finishing projects, always known for putting things down only to pick them back up again months or even years later.

I decided this time would be different. I decided this book will be finished, so if you are reading this now I have managed to achieve that; a giant personal hurdle for myself, and hopefully one that will get the mental ball rolling to make a difference for some of you reading this.

Through having conversations with others, it quickly became apparent that there are many people out there who are deeply unhappy. Everyone is unhappy for a different reason, some have lost their direction, require medical help, feel trapped, unfulfilled, unloved and unsupported, or are dealing with grief. The truth is there are a number of reasons that somebody may be unhappy.

After realising that I'm far from the only one who has gone through struggles, I decided to connect with others and begin to understand some of the reasons for their unhappiness. All of this reinforced my need to want to finish this book on happiness and wellbeing, whilst ensuring I practiced what I preached and built these methods into my daily life; or at least the ones that worked for me. On top of that, I have become a mental health first aider to help signpost others and plan on furthering my study of psychology. Having met many people working within the mental health field, they are some of the most wholesome and grounded people I have had the pleasure of spending time around. Full of healthy habits and advice, as well as practicing the methods they suggest themselves.

If you are ready to start making positive changes and changing 'negative' habits out for 'positive' ones, then by reading this book I hope you can start to change how you think and your perspective of life. Sometimes it may not be your habits that make you unhappy; it may be learning to stand up for yourself and knowing when to say "No" when you need to. Remember, you are not a doormat. A line I often say to those that allow others to emotionally walk all over them. You have needs too, and if they are not being met you will begin to become deeply unhappy. Often the more anxious of us will bend over backwards to try and accommodate our partner's needs, there isn't necessarily an issue with this if you are both meeting in the middle, but one sided compromise can be painful and unfulfilling.

If you are the one that is providing the energy to a friendship or relationship and you stop being the first to message and make plans, instead reciprocating the energy you receive, you may see it for what it is, not what it could be. Perhaps the two of you are different and the only thing keeping you together was the effort and love that you have been providing. That is okay, it is painful and difficult but it is a part of life. People who grow with us are more likely to remain in our lives, those who do not grow or grow in a different direction are meant for different things. If you can stop trying to see the potential in others and accepting them for who they are now, does this change how you think about the situation?

Forcing a situation to work by pouring love and energy into it is draining at best, and damaging to your mental health at worst. This can apply to different situations in life, not just friendships or relationships. If you find you are the one pouring energy and love into something that is not working, you are losing a little bit more of yourself each day that passes. You already know it is not right, but you have not found the courage to say goodbye. The unknown is scary, but being exactly where you are in 20 years' time is terrifying, better to experience temporary discomfort for future comfort. Instant gratification is a distraction from making choices that you will thank yourself for in the future, we all have our vices. Think of it this way, going to the gym today will have you feeling better next week than eating a whole tub of ice cream.

What I'm hoping to achieve by writing this book is that the people I cannot speak to, I can start to get you really thinking about your own happiness and how to start building a happier life around you, one where you make choice that prioritise your wellbeing. I'm hoping this book helps you to take the first steps, to build healthier habits and to try and adjust the way you look at things. This book, or any book, isn't going to cure you or solve all of your problems; only you can do that, but it may give you the tools you need to start making those changes to help build a happier life and to care less about the things that don't really matter.

I am extremely passionate about mental health, promoting positive habits and lifestyle changes. There is an obvious need in the current world full of daily stress and the internet constantly reminding us how unhappy we are, when compared to the picture perfect lives we see online, as well as setting us unrealistic expectations that honestly most of us are never going to meet.

It is important to acknowledge that we are all different and one method that works for me may not work for you, most information I give will be fairly general for this reason, because we are all so different. Our mental health is unique to each of us as individuals, but having someone to talk to and who understands what you are going through is vital to all of us. No matter how tough you think that you are we all need at least that; a therapist, a GP, a psychiatrist, or initially a friend.

One thing I will mention is that you can overburden your friends or significant others. They are not here to fix you, try not to drain them completely, the same goes for you. If you are finding someone incredibly draining, remember they are responsible for their own happiness and that you are responsible for yours. If you need to prioritise your own happiness first that is OK, if you are in a relationship then taking care of your own happiness for yourself and your partner's sake is vital.

You cannot solve everyone else's problems; they have to take accountability for that. We can lend an ear and a guiding hand, but we ultimately cannot change someone else. The domino effect is real; those with poor mental health can negatively affect others by draining them dry. Only when your cup is full are you able to offer from your own, this goes for those around you too. If you are draining them too much they may start to resent you for it; I've been on both ends of this, both the one with a full cup and the one with an empty cup draining others. If you cannot set healthy boundaries it is imperative that you begin to start practicing this, start with small things you can say no to; it becomes much easier once practiced to say no to the bigger things, or to say no to certain types of behaviour.

We are going to delve into different methods to be productive, trying to find your passion, strategies for working outside of your comfort zone, being aware of our mental health, practice being present, trying to look at what we have, not what we don't have, building resilience, some experiences of my own and what really makes you happy and learning to stop caring about the useless stuff.

If you haven't found your passion, or at least something that allows for you to grow as a person (this is also extremely important and will be talked about more in-depth later on) then this is the perfect place to start, by the end of this book I hope to have you thinking about what really makes you happy and some ways to improve your happiness and life.

So without further ado, let's jump into the real stuff. Approach each section with an open mind; see what you can discover about yourself in the process of reading and working through section by section. If you're not at least open to trying different exercises and having an open mind, then you won't change easily. Consistency and patience is key, there is no overnight fix. This is hard to get used to, uncomfortable to begin with and difficult to maintain; but once you start changing it becomes much easier to change our other habits and views to more positive ones.

A happy life looks different for each person, so let's begin by trying to understand what you are happy with and unhappy with in your life. By breaking your life down into smaller segments you can start to take a look at what works just fine, what you would like to change and what you can change.

Chapter 2

The Iceberg

Let me introduce to you a guy I knew. From the outside, he has a lot going right for him, surrounded by friends and family, a respectable job and what seems like a loving partner, but like many of us he is an emotional iceberg.

What you don't see above the surface is that he is deeply unhappy, his anger has been getting worse over time and he is becoming snappier at home, he works a job he can't wait to escape each day and struggles to focus when he is there. His friends never seem to get him and are always telling him how lucky he is and how they wish their life was better or more like his, but when he compares himself to the celebrities and models he sees on social media he doesn't feel that way, he just feels like a failure that is unable to fulfil his potential. He begins to drink more on the weekends and spends less time doing the things that he used to enjoy.

When he looks in the mirror all he sees is how fat he looks compared to the Instagram models, but by most standards he is mildly-overweight at best, his girlfriend and friends say they think his 'dad bod' is cute, but he has always daydreamed about having a six-pack and ripped body.
He posts topless pictures of himself, statuses and stories saying how happy and lucky he is, but this is all for show, an ego boost and for likes on social media. If anything, this is having a negative effect on him.
After a while he ends up having a breakdown, the stress becomes

too much and he ends up quitting his job, escaping his partner and leaving behind the life he had.

The thing is he never felt understood by the people around him, neither by his friends or family. He was surrounded by people but felt alone, unhappy in his work, emotionally abused in his relationship and misunderstood by those around him, and it all became too much. He begins a stream of impulsive decisions, quitting his job, moving away from his parents, turning to alcohol and self-harm, perhaps to mask his problems and his inability to cope with how he feels.

This story isn't all that uncommon, but this is my story, a younger me who suffered to the point of depression and a breakdown. Triggered predominantly by an emotionally abusive relationship, along with issues I had been refusing to confront; some of the scars I have only just begun to unwrap and understand now.

When we feel isolated and misaligned it's easy to feel lonely in a sea of people. If you don't connect with the people that are around you, loneliness and unhappiness can soon follow. Working in a job that you hate will leave you unfulfilled and empty inside, it doesn't matter how much it pays. Money doesn't buy happiness, a certain level of security will help how you feel as Maslow (1954) illustrates with his hierarchy of needs, but after a certain point it won't add further quality to your life; just different problems.

Below we have the hierarchy of needs, a well-known representation of what you as a human require to thrive. In order for this to occur, the essentials have to be met, such as safety, food, sleep and enough to get by. Only once these basic needs are met, you can you begin to focus on the other aspects of life that bring a sense of purpose and belonging. As you can see, money brings a certain level of security but once this has been attained there are other needs that we have as humans too, belonging and esteem can become hampered by comparing yourself to others.

Social media posting is one way in which you and I may try to meet this need, the better the post does with likes and comments the greater the sense of enhancement you are likely to feel to your self-esteem. Whilst negative comments or feedback could damage your mental health and make you more susceptible to emotional distress (Beyari, 2023). Depending upon how social media is used, it can have a very negative effect on wellbeing and self-image, especially for those spending a lot of time on social media (Zsila & Reyes, 2023).

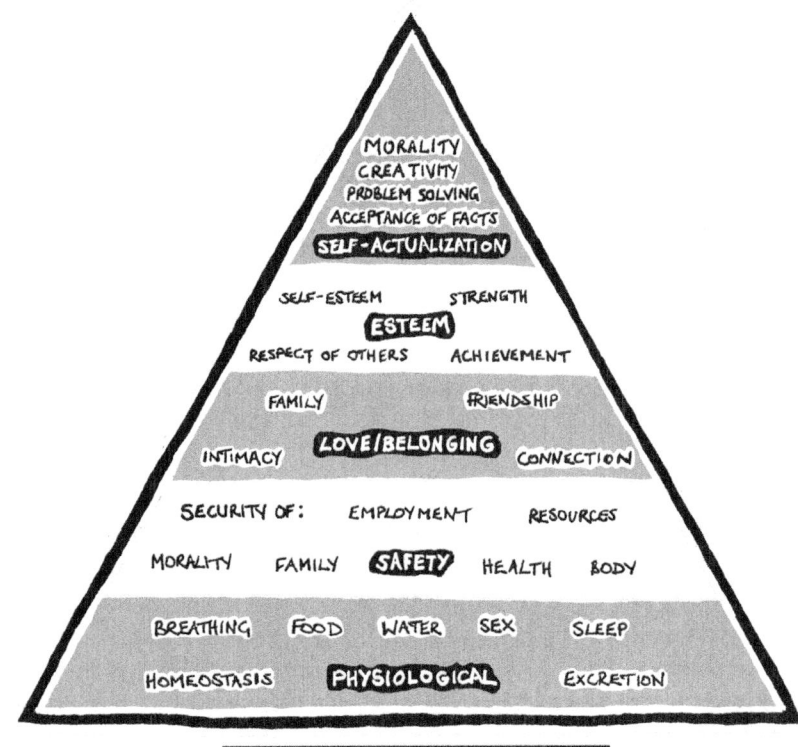

Social media in the modern world is a common culprit for comparison, perfect bodies, perfect lives, perfect **everything**. Let's be honest, social media is like an emotional iceberg, you only see what you are shown. You see about 10% of what is actually there, the other 90% of someone's life we have no idea what is going on, but if you keep on comparing yourself to the lives of others, it will eventually sink you.

For those that are trying to maintain an image on social media, constantly pretending will eventually take its toll on you, when the façade can no longer be kept up and people reach their limits, something has to give. We often see people have breakdowns or a mid-life crisis as a result of stress building up, uncertainty, and the sensation of feeling trapped or poor mental health, just like me.

Social media and high levels of screen time may be one of the contributing factors of this; thirty years ago you would compare yourself against those in your friendship group, town or city. Now, it is easy to compare yourself against top athletes, film stars, and celebrities with a few swipes of a finger. It has never been easier to see what is lacking and to idolize what others have with a mentality of "the grass is always greener", all this means is that you are busy looking at what others have and fantasising about it. But the truth is the grass is greener wherever you water it, your garden can be the best fucking garden in the world if you tend to it, it just takes some work.

Using social media to gain a sense of belonging and to boost your self-esteem is a dangerous game to play, curating the best aspects of your life to create an online persona is exhausting. Believing everything you see on social media can be damaging to both wellbeing and self-image, and passive activity on social media such as reading posts is more strongly associated with depression than active use such as making them (Karim et al., 2020).

We can set ourselves unrealistic expectations when we compare ourselves to others on social media, dreaming of a life we may never have. Too much dreaming and fantasizing allows for a romantic dream, a perfect picture you can live in your head, but without action you will never make it a reality. We all too often forget that life is always full of problems; we just have to choose the ones we want to deal with. That perfect life you imagine you want to live probably isn't as perfect as you think. Just full of different problems, but still full of problems, that's the thing with life. It's never easy, nor should it be.

How you spend your limited time in life is vitally important, we only have so long on this earth and time is something we cannot claw back. If you are hoping to fulfil your hopes and dreams, then you may have to sacrifice in some other areas of your life. Most of us have 4000 weeks to live our life, and that's if we're lucky, so how are you going to spend your precious weeks? The average person spends 2.3 hours a day on social media platforms, which is a lot when you add it up over time (Zsila & Reyes, 2023).

If you find yourself endlessly scrolling through Instagram, Facebook, Tiktok, Youtube or other social media platforms, then perhaps it is time you start creating more time for yourself. It is easy to fall into an endless trap of screen time, and often by the end of it you haven't achieved anything, just more screen time. A review of studies looking at the effect of electronic media on teenagers found a correlation between increased social media time and poor self-esteem, reduced life satisfaction and unhappiness (Abi-Jaoude et al., 2020). Another review of literature found social media as a risk factor for teenagers, increasing the risk behaviours such as alcohol consumption, drug, tobacco, gambling and taking sexual risks (Purba et al., 2023). If you are going to use these platforms, try to use them for more positive reasons such as connecting with friends and family or joining causes that are important to you, which may have a more positive effect on your mind (Vaingankar et al., 2022).

In the modern world, happiness seems to be an after-thought, left behind or pushed to the side for many. With a lot of people taking the approach that "just getting on with it", or "fake it 'till you make it" is the only way forward. Fortunately, this is a load of rubbish. In the aftermath of the global pandemic, many more people have started to put their happiness first. It did, however, take a global catastrophe for many people to start thinking about this; sometimes a catalyst for change is required and it isn't always pretty. This can be the fuel to enable you to change habits, situations or challenge ways of thinking.

More people have started to acknowledge the fact that "Money can't buy you happiness". In fact, some of those in the higher earning bracket may actually be *more* unhappy than those earning a lower or average salary (Kudrna & Kushlev, 2022). People are starting to wake up to the fact that being unhappy doesn't have to be ignored anymore and accepted as the status quo. If you are not happy with your life, it doesn't have to stay this way.

Why settle for a job, situation or person in your life that makes you feel *wrong*? It may be a lingering doubt in your mind or perhaps you've known for a while but just don't know how to change the situation. You wouldn't buy a house that you didn't like, so why would you settle for a job that you hate, a situation that makes your life miserable, or people that dampen your mood whenever you're around them? Perhaps you are not unhappy for any of these reasons, it may be a thought in the back of your mind that you were meant for more, that you deserve more in life and that not being able to achieve that is making you feel behind and not where you want to be. Maybe you regret never taking that chance you had earlier in life and dwell on what could have been if you chose a different path, or it might be something much simpler like balancing your own needs with the needs of others.

I'm not saying you have to be as impulsive and gung-ho as me, but sometimes you have to take a leap of faith. Your risk tolerance, dependants and your financial situation will determine how much of a risk you can take without putting yourself through unnecessary stress. It's important to remember that financial stresses can negatively impact you when you are struggling to pay bills and get by.

It is important to prioritise your own needs, don't give the opinions of others too much notice as this can hold you back from your true calling and full potential. Caring less about the opinions of others can free you from the mental shackles that bind you, what I mean by that is not giving a toss helps to emotionally unburden you, and man does that feel good. If you choose to use social media, acknowledging that it could negatively affect you is important. "Doomscrolling", the act of continuing to scroll despite the fact the content may be negative, as well as passively using social media platforms to consume huge amounts of information could lead to anxiety or depression (Satici et al., 2022).

If there is one quality about myself that I am glad that I possess, it is that if I am unhappy, I will either leave or change a situation until I no longer feel that way. If you take a quick look at my CV it is easy to see at a glance that I job hop. Now employers don't like to see too much of this, so I've had to be intelligent about how I presented my CV to would-be-employers. It's part of the game, we all do it to some extent. So long as you can get the job, are willing to learn new skills and have at least some of the required ones, you'll do just fine. If you are lazy and unwilling to learn, this is going to show straight away. Skills can be taught, but personality and enthusiasm are for you to bring along.

This has taken a fair few years of trial and error, and has resulted in some pretty extreme decisions during my life so far.
From trying to survive on Universal Credit, by scraping by on a mere £500 a month, starting my own businesses, taking risks on investments, leaving jobs I hated at the expense of financial security, and doing what was necessary to put my health and wellbeing before finances and niceties.

However, I can honestly say that I am a much happier human as a result of these decisions and remember, happiness to me is priceless. It's extremely liberating when you are in control of your life and able to influence your surroundings and environment. Real happiness is not just about the emotion happiness, but about being able to shape and change your life to a better one you are happy living. By caring less about the things that do not matter, you can start to care more about the things that do and prioritise your wellbeing.

The idea of this book is to give you some insight into decisions I have taken, and how you can use that information to better your own happiness and change your circumstances to improve your quality of life and wellbeing. Ranging from what you enjoy doing, to some real reflection about what makes you happy as a person. Each chapter will aim to provoke your thoughts, question the way you think and have some actions for you to put to the test yourself.

Happiness looks different to everybody; we each have our own version of it, hopefully this book starts to get you thinking about your own happiness and how to cultivate it.

The Happiness Hormones

In order to cultivate it, understanding the science behind happiness and the hormones responsible for making you feeling happy are essential. Dopamine, serotonin, endorphins and oxytocin are needed in order to feel happy and for us to function normally.

Let's take a quick look at each of these and how they play a role in a normal day for us, dopamine is linked to our reward and motivation system, receive a compliment at work? That's dopamine you feel. Win on a scratch card? Yup, you guessed it, dopamine. Received a lot of likes on a social media post? You see where this is going. Not every person will receive a dopamine release for the same activities, as we're all different so are our causes for release, however, generally activities that are more addictive generate a higher release for the general population.

That's not to say something has to be addictive to trigger a release, as it also links to our motivation system. A variety of activities can also boost your dopamine levels, including food, sex, exercise and any activity that you enjoy. Without this essential hormone feelings of apathy can creep in, making you sluggish and disinterested in activities you ordinarily would enjoy.
There are also thought to be possible gut-brain links, which could suggest that what you eat plays a role in what you feel and the progression of conditions such as Parkinson's' (Franko et al., 2021).

Serotonin is the ***true*** happiness hormone, or neurotransmitter, responsible for long lasting feelings of happiness, sleep regulation, mood and digestion. Ways to increase serotonin levels naturally include eating foods rich in tryptophan, reducing stress levels, exercising and increasing your exposure to sunlight. A serotonin imbalance can affect the processing of emotions, whilst low levels of dopamine can cause feelings of hopelessness and a lack of interest in activities (Bamalan et al., 2023).

Disruption to your serotonin levels are a probable cause for depression, many medications for depression target serotonin specifically. Known as Selective Serotonin Reuptake Inhibitors (SSRIs) they actively reduce the re-uptake levels of serotonin meaning you have higher levels present in your brain, to help keep your serotonin levels closer to where they should be.
The issue is that breakthrough symptoms can occur, where despite being medicated symptoms persist or reappear, generally resulting in a dose change or medication adjustment. On top of this there are a number of side-effects, some of which

include causing anxiety, depression and suicidal thoughts. Sounds crazy, right? Stopping them abruptly or missing doses can cause withdrawal symptoms, ranging from hyper-arousal to hallucinations and anxiety (Chiappini et al., 2022).

Endorphins are released during activities that cause stress, pleasurable activities or when your body feels pain. Exercise is a common trigger for the release of endorphins and perhaps one of the healthier ways to enable a release, sex, eating and massage can also do the same. However, any activity that causes pain can cause a release, such as emotional pain, physical pain, stress or intentional physical pain such as self-harm. This inhibiting-neurotransmitter is responsible for allowing us to push through physical limitations by dulling neurological pain receptors. Some may know this is the "Runners High", which can be triggered after about four miles of running, enabling us to push through with a new sense of energy.

Last of the four is oxytocin, often referred to as the love hormone due to the mechanisms of release, which include kissing, hugging, sex, healthy interactions with friends, massage or physical contact of the skin. It can have positive effects such as reducing cortisol, which is responsible for stress, as well as the lowering of your blood pressure. Both are fantastic ways to help you feel more relaxed and calm, if you ever wondered why you felt good after having a really enjoyable day with friends this could be one of the hormones responsible for the sensation (Ito et al., 2019).

Similarly, when we are attracted to somebody our body releases a surge of dopamine, serotonin levels increase and oxcytocin is released, this can be why we feel such a rush of positive emotions when we like somebody; often resulting in the honeymoon phase, especially early on in a relationship or new romantic connection. Every little interaction with this person can release a steady stream of dopamine, and this phase is essential in order for us to build trust and connection with our new romantic partner.

So there we have the four key players when it comes to your happiness and some examples of when they are released or levels increase. Any disruption to just one of these hormones can be catastrophic to our wellbeing; if parts of the brain that release or control these are altered then how we feel can dramatically change. There are a number of reasons that things can get out of whack, but looking after your health gives you a fighting fit chance of being able to regulate your hormones better. From what you eat, to the drugs you take, how much sleep you get, how much sunlight you get, how much alcohol you drink, and your exercise levels all play a vital role in how you feel overall.

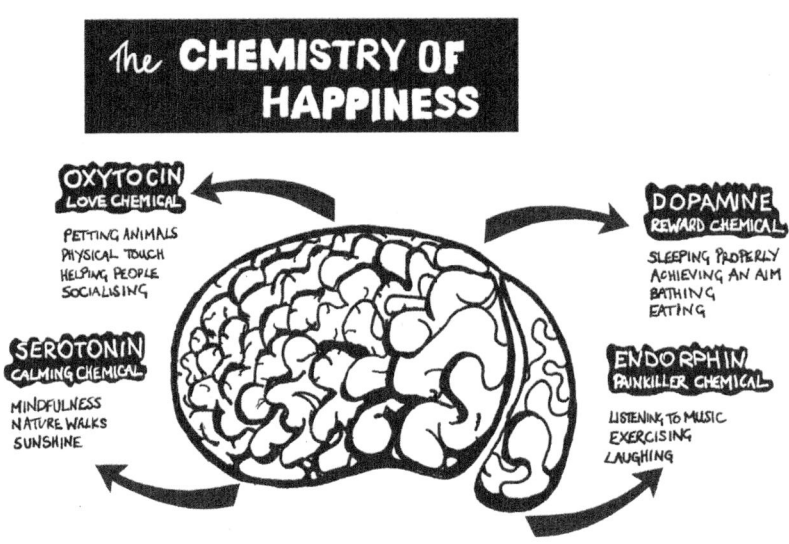

There are all sorts of factors that can put you at increased risk of feeling unhappy, medical conditions, a diet lacking in nutrients, the inability to process vitamins or nutrients, swelling, brain tumours, or anything affecting your brain in a negative way that can alter the normal release of hormones and ultimately how you feel. Happiness is simple in principle, but if the reality was that simple many more of us would feel happy and content each day.

Now that you have a basic understanding of the four hormones, or neurotransmitters, responsible for the feelings of happiness, the rest of the book will look at ways to naturally increase these. As well as some of the obstacles that can get in your way, such as poor mental health, addiction, and an unhealthy lifestyle and high stress levels. Stress is a nightmare, and as it can inhibit the release of some of these hormones that we need, it's definitely something you want to try and reduce if it is starting to spill into other areas of your life.

Chapter 3

Ikigai: What Does Happiness Look Like To You?

The thing with happiness is that it is personal to each and every one of us. One person's happiness will most certainly be different to another's. As each and every one of us is different, so is our happiness and what makes us feel content and fulfilled. You may have a friend who loves numbers, one that loves design, singing, dancing, cooking, or something completely different to what you enjoy. The key point here is that what makes one person happy isn't necessarily going to make another happy. There are common feelings and needs that need to be met; these are often similar, but how you meet those needs is different for each person.

This is where you have to really sit down and learn about yourself, what makes you happy? What makes you tick? Is there something specific that is making you unhappy? Can you pinpoint why it makes you unhappy? Try writing these things down to help you focus on the positives and negatives, it can help with the overall picture and how you really feel about a situation or your current circumstances.

Some hobbies can end up becoming a job, or a side-gig that makes money for you alongside your day job. If you are in the position of wanting to start a new venture to earn money, that is more in line with your values and beliefs, then this section may be for you.

I have found the best way to pinpoint what you enjoy is to figure out what you are good at and also look at what you naturally spend your time doing. Finding a compromise or a half-way can sometimes be healthy, if you turn your passion into a job there is always a risk that you will find it a chore and lose the love for it. Try looking at what activities you excel at, both skills and personality traits, and then identifying what aspects you enjoy of this and then go from there.

Placing boundaries for yourself can be good here, the thing you are passionate about and enjoy may not become the thing you pursue in life, but it could become the hobby that you enjoy in your spare time. What activities make the day fly by when you do them? The one that has you forgetting to take breaks and when you look up five hours later realise you still haven't eaten, the thing you get lost in and enjoy. When this occurs it is often referred to as a state of flow, when you are undertaking a challenging but enjoyable activity that you perform well in, flow can be experienced.

Now in terms of what activities are right for you, that's for you to explore. Ah the great joy of exploring.

Perhaps you enjoy exercise and staying healthy, but you wouldn't want to become a nutritionist or a personal trainer because you enjoy your own personal development rather than building and developing others; perhaps this is how you switch off. There is nothing wrong with this, but you have to learn about yourself and understand what you do and do not want to do.

If you are someone that has lots of different interests and hobbies, one way to approach this is pick three hobbies: one that you do for money, one you do for pleasure and one that is creative and fulfilling to help you express yourself. You can always re-evaluate if making money out of one of the hobbies has taken all the fun away from it, perhaps this hobby isn't the goldmine.

When you are trying to choose a hobby that could potentially make money, there are a few different aspects that you need to consider. I find that breaking the hobby down is useful, ask the following questions and be honest:

> *a) Do you enjoy it? If you don't enjoy your work it will show to others.*
>
> *b) Are you good at it? Good enough that others would purchase from you or want to learn from you?*
>
> *c) Is there a market for this? If there is no market and people aren't willing to spend money on this, then perhaps it's not the money-maker.*
>
> *d) Does the world need this? Is this going to benefit others in a positive manner?*

This can separate a hobby from a potential business opportunity. Ideally, you are looking to tick all four of the above. Usually the things that we enjoy we are also good at, but we don't generally start off good at everything. In fact, we usually suck to begin with, this is why practice is important and seeing what you naturally spend your time on can help to identify what you enjoy.

For me personally, I love to cook. During my spare time you will often find me cooking up new dishes or trying recipes, but the funny thing is when I tried cooking as a job I didn't enjoy it. It turns out I enjoy creative cooking for myself and friends; rather than a set menu for customers.

Becoming self-aware when it comes to your work life can be very liberating, some people know what they want to do their whole life, and then there are those of us who never really know. Neither is wrong, but when you feel no sense of purpose and direction it can be very difficult to direct your energy efficiently. It is also theorised that having a sense of purpose greater than yourself can positively benefit your wellbeing in the long run.

This is why balancing your passions versus your work life can be important, for me I learned that some things are best kept as a hobby and not to be pursued as a job. Perhaps in the future I'll explore a different avenue that allows for creativity but also doesn't feel like work. For now, food stays as a hobby and that's just fine.

Ikigai

The Japanese Ikigai framework is an excellent visual illustration that can help to identify the work you are good at, what you love, what the world needs and what you can be paid for.

Ikigai roughly translates to "reason for being", your purpose, why you are here. The word 'Iki' meaning life and the word 'Gai' means purpose, meaning or values, think of it as the thing that gets you out of bed every day. Essentially, this is your calling in life.

Having an Ikigai, or purpose, has been shown to promote health and wellbeing among Japanese older adults, decreasing depressive symptoms, reduced helplessness, as well as boosting levels of life satisfaction and happiness (Okuzono et al., 2022).

So the research seems to suggest that it can have a positive effect, but how do you find it?

What does that actually look like to a normal person like you and me?

Your Ikigai is composed of Passion, Mission, Profession and Vocation, these four aspects aligning to ultimately be your life's purpose, the thing that brings you satisfaction, fullness, excitement and comfort. It may be you are still on the path of discovering what your Ikigai looks like, for many this can take years, or perhaps you are already pursuing it with a sense of purpose and excitement.

If you struggle creating a list of activities and passions, perhaps it is time to try new things in life, to help you find your 'Ikigai'. You have to give things a chance in life, by exposing yourself to new and interesting hobbies it could be you find out much more about yourself than you thought possible. This is by no means a quick and easy journey; it can take people their whole lives to find their calling.

You are never too old to try something new, this is a point I cannot stress enough to anybody reading this right now. No matter how old you are, you are still young enough to do something you have always wanted to do, or never done before. There is no time limit on trying new things.

There are whole books that focus solely on Ikigai, some of them are fantastic reads if you want to delve into the topic much deeper, such as **"Ikigai: The Japanese secret to a long and happy life"** by Hector Garcia and Francesc Miralles. I won't be covering it in much more detail than this, but the importance is to understand that if you have not tried new experiences, vocations and activities then it will be much more difficult to find. Those who have found their Ikigai or true calling are in a better position to be happier, this isn't a guarantee but work makes up such a huge portion of most peoples' lives that getting out of bed every day with purpose and passion can really drive you forwards. Ikigai doesn't even have to be the work you do, but the purpose that you serve, the thing you love doing with a sense of accomplishment and fulfilment along the way.

This is where you have to really hone in what you enjoy, what is your idea of happiness? Are you looking to work long hours at a job you love, or have the freedom to work and travel at the same time? What makes you, well, you? If you are struggling to pick out what you are good at versus what you enjoy, try asking someone close to you. More often than not they will know what you are good at by seeing you in a way that you are unable to see yourself.

Here is a little activity for you to try if you are struggling to pinpoint what you enjoy and are skilled at.

Start by writing down things you both like to do or are skilled in. Then break these down even further, what exactly is it that you enjoy about that particular activity? Can you break it down even further again and say why you enjoy it; does it make you feel a sense of achievement; or to help you relax? Or is there another reason that you like to undertake it?

This will only help you get to know yourself better. Once you have done this, well done! This is actually an incredibly difficult first step to take, but it should have helped to give you some ideas about what you enjoy, what you are good at and why you enjoy a particular activity.

Let me give you a little example to get you started and guide you, taking writing as an example.

I enjoy writing because I'm good at it, it doesn't feel like work and some would say I have a bit of a knack for it. Most importantly it's easy for me, it comes as second nature. Whilst I'm not very artistic I'm quite creative, and writing allows for me to create words with no limitations that I otherwise find a brush and paints impose. ***It feels nice to write down thoughts and to be able to pass those thoughts onto other people in a way that can educate or express them.***

To delve even further, I enjoy it because I set the pace I work at. I'm bad at pressure and stressful situations and writing generally doesn't create a situation like this which keeps me within my comfort zone, whilst also pushing creative boundaries. It also challenges me, I'm poor when it comes to being consistent and this is something that helps me to track consistency and for me to be more dedicated to a project.

This activity is incredibly powerful and can be done over, and over and over again to help you really dive into you as a person and to help you further understand yourself.

If you get stuck, don't worry. It can take a little time to adjust to this way of thinking but writing stuff down does help, it enables you to really focus on understanding your feelings and thoughts surrounding a situation or choice. If you just leave them in your head, thoughts and feelings can get a little confusing, by projecting them onto paper it helps to solidify an idea or emotion much better to help you understand what you are thinking and feeling.

This is perfect for not only understanding but making it real. Many of us escape by ignoring problems in our life, by writing down what you are feeling, you bring it into reality, it's better to confront than ignore problems. Taking active steps to recognize and being more self-aware can be incredibly powerful. Reflection is often done this way to help you evaluate a situation and to break down elements into smaller pieces.

To begin with you are probably going to suck at whatever your chosen hobby is, people may not acknowledge your work or progress, just remember who you are doing it for. Steven King didn't start out a best-selling author, in fact he struggled for a long time to become published, working the graveyard shift at a hotel where he used to write as much as he could. His book on writing talks about his breakthrough novel Carrie, and how his partner fished it out of the bin covered in cigarette ash, only to be encouraged by her that he had to publish this masterpiece. Guess what? He did, and it started off what was possibly one of the most successful writing careers out there.

The Beatles were another example, before coming to fame they were seen as a bunch of long-haired hippies in Liverpool, which my great granddad reminded them, as he chased them out of his front room they were practicing in before heading off to Europe. If he had known they would turn out to be one of the greatest bands of their era; would he have still chased them calling them long-haired hippies? Who knows, maybe he would have, but they were once upon a time a band that nobody had really heard of.

One of your hobbies could lead down a similar route, if you follow your passion or Ikigai. Who knows, the possibilities are limitless.

Try picking three hobbies or interests you have and use the above method to identify which of the three you could potentially turn into a money-maker, which one makes you happy, and which one is your creative outlet in life. Sometimes the creative outlet becomes the money-maker, just go with whatever comes naturally.

To find your Ikigai you will ultimately find a purpose that combines many aspects that you enjoy and find fulfilling, having a purpose in life, something greater than yourself to accomplish can keep you going during the hard times.

If you haven't got three hobbies or interests, then be sure to read the next chapter and start taking action to change this.

Chapter 4

Finding Your Passion Through Doing

Finding your passion may not be as simple as writing things down that you enjoy. The truth is, if you are young or haven't explored much of the world you may still be searching for your passion. After all, you have to try new things to discover what you like and dislike. Nobody else can do this for you, so getting out there and exploring is the first step to take on this journey.

If trying new activities or learning new skills is something that you find particularly difficult, set yourself a goal or try it along with a friend to help boost your motivation. By trying an activity with a friend it can make you directly accountable to somebody else and not just yourself. This is especially useful when trying new things, as a lot of people are anxious or shy when trying an activity with others for the first time. If you go along with a friend you can suck at said activity and be new together, or if you have a friend that is experienced then they should be able to show you the basics and help your confidence.

There are all sorts of thing you may try, such as dancing, rock climbing, biking, learning a language, art classes, writing, drawing, sailing, or developing a skill such as day trading or even training for a new profession. There is literally no limit to the activities that you may enjoy and could even end up being something you consider a passion. The important thing is to make an effort to try something new, without trying how can you know?

You could even find that something you never imagined you would enjoy turns out to be the very thing you love. Whatever it is, give it a go before you write it off. I have found trying new classes or starting up a new hobby is a great way to discover more about myself and what I do and do not enjoy, as well as being a good means of making friends who enjoy the same hobby as you.

If you don't try to broaden your horizons, it may take much longer to find your passion and ultimately your Ikigai, if this is something you are striving to find. By actively making an effort to expand your comfort zone and delve into what you do enjoy versus things you do not enjoy, you can really start to see a contrast and also learn more about yourself in the process.

This might be something that you enjoy doing, and you want to do it for the sake of enjoyment, or maybe you are challenging yourself to try new things and wish to push past your usual comfort into the growth and learning zone.

Whatever the reason may be, trying something new doesn't have to be scary. There are ways to turn it into a positive experience that you will enjoy. The thing is if you haven't found your true passion yet, it could be just around the corner. This doesn't just apply for finding things that you enjoy; this applies to all situations in life. We rarely know what is right around the corner and when opportunities are presented it can be good to pick those that align with your ethos and values.

If you are currently unhappy in your life and what you are doing, branch out. Explore different areas of life, as the chances are that if you are unhappy with what you are doing for work or your current situation, you aren't actively doing the right things for yourself.

When we are doing something that is not right; that is to say not aligning with what we enjoy and believe in, we can begin to feel trapped. Humans are fickle creatures; once we begin to feel trapped or we lose a sense of control we can begin to feel unhappy each day. It's easy to feel trapped in a situation when you feel as if you have to continue doing what you are now, with no clear route out. Remember to peak your head out of your current situation to give yourself a reality check – you are not stuck, you are just not looking outside of your current situation. There is always a way to move in a different direction, it may just seem daunting at first.

When you are feeling stressed, emotional or trapped you often have a narrow line of sight, with the whole picture being obscured. If you can take a more objective view, or a rational view, it usually becomes apparent things aren't quite as hopeless as you first thought. "Take three steps back", a line my girlfriend often reminds me when I am feeling overwhelmed or having irrational thoughts.

Trying new things and branching out is an excellent way to break this vicious cycle of emotional tunnel vision, it enables you to not to feel as trapped to begin with and instead helps to build and develop you as a person. Personal growth is an incredibly powerful tool, and many people stagnate and forget to focus on this aspect of themselves during the busy day-to-day of life.

Actively taking some time for you to try new activities or to learn new skills is an incredibly positive action, humans are designed to learn, adapt and develop themselves further; essentially allowing for us to survive as a species. If you neglect this action, you will likely find yourself bored and not feeling challenged by life. Maybe it's time you started to challenge yourself in other ways.

I personally took about a year of actively trying new activities and clubs to meet new people and keep me busy, I tried two different forms of dancing along with branching out into trying to learn some photo and video editing skills. You can start small and expand into areas that you enjoy, I decided dancing wasn't for me, but it was fun to try out. Video and photo editing however turned into both a useful and enjoyable skill, opening up a whole new avenue I had never explored before.

If you find that you are struggling for ideas when it comes to activities or clubs to try, try asking your friends or family and see what they like to do in their spare time. By trying things with others you are more likely to stick at it and on top of this you can get stuck in immediately by going along or joining in on their hobby. The advantage of this is that you have someone to introduce you to the activity and will not have to seek out something on your own. However, if you aren't a fan of this idea then it may be time to start searching your local area to see what is on offer.

Places that are good for seeing what is on offer in the local area include, local Facebook groups, local magazines, the library (I know, this may sound dated but a lot of clubs advertise in places such as this) or Google; a simple "What clubs and activities are in my area?" can go a long way. Failing this, ask a friend or colleague what is on offer locally. The right thing for you may be entirely different to them, so start to branch out and explore new avenues of interest.

A lot of people dream of becoming a successful Youtuber or Instagram influencer, video and photo editing skills are directly useful to branching out into this area. With technology continuing to advance and smart phones becoming a social normality, having the skills to record and edit content, market it, and create digital art are in higher demand than ever. Whilst it is important to acknowledge the effects that social media can have on your mental health, there are ways to use it for creative content which is thought provoking and educational for others.

One of the benefits that becoming absorbed in a hobby or task is that you forget about yourself and can get completely lost in what you are doing. It could be music, art, design, a sport – so long as it is something that you enjoy and can get lost in for hours at a time; often referred to as 'flow'.

Just by speaking to colleagues and seeing what hobbies they had, I found out one guy was going to a martial arts class, another was an artist on the side and the others got up to things I would never had thought to do in my spare time. Speaking and communicating with others may help you to find the right activity or skill to try for yourself. You never know where you may end up and what new hobbies or passions you could discover. The key is to be bold; if you are not willing to try new things then you will not be able to expand your horizons. If you are not willing to try new things, how are you going to make bigger changes in your life later on?

Start small, take up a new hobby; it could be a group hobby or one that you use to keep yourself distracted from the world's worries for a few hours. You can have as many hobbies as you like, but if you want to be good at them, or are limited on time then picking just a handful may be a better approach. This is not to say you should not try new hobbies now and again, in fact I highly suggest trying different activities to keep your life varied. Creative hobbies in particular can be a fantastic outlet for your mental health and as a source of expression; there are many different mediums for being creative; not just paint and canvas.

Once you have found something that you enjoy, start becoming good at it. Personally, I like to have an active hobby, a relaxing hobby and then a creative one. If you want to you can turn any of these into a career, but not everybody wants to do that. For me that looks like going to the gym, cooking, gaming, investing and currently writing, this will change over time and depending upon how I feel. Notice how I have a few things I use to relax?

There is also the potential to turn these hobbies into profitable ventures if I wanted to; I could become a personal trainer, start an educational Youtube channel, write blog posts about exercise, gaming or cooking, create a recipe book, courses, content about finance, a game, or write reviews for games. There are multitudes of ways you can turn a hobby into a career, it all starts with you enjoying it and then deciding if turning it profitable is right for you, or if the enjoyment you get from it is enough.

Want to know what is even better? Creative hobbies have been shown to have possible links to improved mental health; one study by Davies et al. (2016) found that those engaging in 100 or more hours a year of arts, or creative activities, for two or more hours a week, reported significantly better mental wellbeing than those that did not. Some food for thought next time you are thinking of a hobby to start.

There is no hard and fast rule, get out there and try broadening your horizons! You might just find the right thing for you.

Chapter 5

Minding Your Mental

It would be irresponsible of me to write a book on happiness without covering some of the harsh realities and conditions that need to be signposted.

Most people spend more time looking after their teeth than their mental health; let that sink in for a minute. Most people spend four minutes a day brushing their teeth, but many of us do not allow this much time to maintain our mental wellbeing. The recommended guidelines for physical exercise are 150 minutes of moderate exercise per week, but the same guidelines are not given for our mental wellbeing. Some kids are now fortunate enough to be taught about the importance of opening up in school, but for those of us no longer in education, what do we do?

We are often not taught the importance of our mental health, we figure out the importance of it during life but how do we look after it, how do we manage something we cannot see? The truth is this is different for everyone, but there are things you can do to build resilience and to better manage stress levels.

A few quick points I would like to make before we start; men have feelings too, we just hide them a lot. Men often don't have people they can talk to, or feel they can talk to. Women can be exactly the same, this isn't just about men. We can all suffer from poor mental health, no matter our age, gender, lifestyle, sexuality or religious beliefs. There is no shame in having poor mental health, but you will have to try to do something about it when you are emotionally ready to.

Mental health, depression and anxiety are difficult subjects to cover. Earlier I mentioned how we are all different, but our problems and issues often aren't so different. How we react in situations differs, but the emotions we feel during a situation can often be more similar than we realise. How often do you talk to someone else about how a situation makes you both feel? I suspect not very often.

After looking at the mental health statistics within the UK, females are more likely to be diagnosed with anxiety or depression (Van de Velde et al., 2010), but men are more likely to die as a result of poor mental health. In fact, according to Statista (2023) from 2000 to 2022 the rate of suicides among males was 16.4 per 100,000 compared to among females which the rate sat at 5.4, meaning males were three times more likely to die by suicide, according to these statistics. Men are also more likely to abuse substances such as drugs or alcohol to deal with their poor mental health. I believe women are better at talking about how they feel in general, whilst a lot of men don't feel like they are allowed to talk about how they are feeling or don't know how to approach the subject. This is just speculation but I think perhaps more women are diagnosed with poor mental health because they actually seek help; men choose not to, or feel unable to.

This may be due to a combination of factors, but often guys feel they need to maintain an alpha or macho stereotype; this is a load of rubbish. Men need to talk just as much as women. So while the number of women being diagnosed with poor mental health is much higher, the number of men that end their life by suicide is unfortunately higher than females. This is not to say women do not attempt suicide; it is often that the methods men use are much more violent and definitive. Either way it is a daunting thing to tackle, but especially if you feel alone a support network can literally save your life. There are studies and papers that show having a support network can boost your oxytocin levels, which may even aid in treating poor mental health (Florea et al., 2022).

Those within the lesbian, gay, bisexual, intersex, queer and transgender community are at an increased risk of self-harm, suicide ideation and poor mental health. Not because of their sexual orientation, but because of bullying, societal exclusion, hate crimes and the nastiness of others. The exact risk factors are not clearly defined when looking at the research, but I do not believe it takes a genius to understand that being marginalized is going to have negative effects on a person's mental wellbeing. It is important to acknowledge that anybody being subject to such discriminatory behaviours is at an increased risk when compared to those not being discriminated against. I believe we have a responsibility to be more understanding and supportive of those that are different to us, however those differences may look, remember that there is a person with feelings at the end of those comments and remarks.

Mental health and wellbeing is incredibly important, in the UK we are only really starting to acknowledge this now. The pandemic highlighted that many people do not have the support systems in place to make it through life. Isolation, loneliness, depression and anxiety have all been heightened in many people, exacerbating the many problems that were already there but had not been addressed.

Talking

For those of you that are deeply unhappy, struggling to get out of bed, struggling to function day-to-day or just barely holding it together before you have a mental breakdown - talk. Talk to a doctor, a family member, a friend, a partner, or anyone you feel comfortable talking to! It is a first step that is scary but crucial to help you get through what is ahead.

The truth is, if you are clinically depressed you are going to need some help and talking to your doctor is the best advice I can give. A doctor may not be the right person for everyone, if you have a negative experience with a medical professional it can put you off. I promise you people do care about you, and the world is not a better place without your light.

Having a mental health illness does not make you a failure or any less human than the next person, having an illness is just that, an illness. A condition that without seeking help can worsen and become debilitating, it is not something you are able to "snap out of" or magically get better from overnight, and it is something you need real genuine assistance with (Behere et al., 2017). There should be absolutely no shame in asking for help, we cannot do everything alone and to think we can is stubborn. You are not burdening other people by trying to get better; you are looking after yourself as you need.

If people go to the doctors for a cough and a cold when they don't need to, do you really think a medical professional will not take your seriously if you book an appointment for something that could be limiting you every day, something that in some instances could not only be holding you back, but putting you at risk of injury or harm?

Many people do not seek early intervention when it comes to mental health. From a 2013 study by Henderson et al. it was identified that globally 70% of people with mental illnesses do not seek treatment from a health care professional. We have moved on from then, but there are still huge barriers to mental health treatment and management, from stigma and discrimination to our own fears of acceptance. We are lucky in the United Kingdom that there are many campaigns and charities trying to reduce the stigma surrounding mental health, but even with all of these it still continues.

Having been there myself, I know how daunting it can be. Acknowledging that you are not OK is a big step to take; taking action is something a lot of us put off, but you have to put yourself first. If you had a broken leg you would see a doctor, so why do we not talk about mental health in the same way? Just because we do not see it as easily as a broken leg, it makes it no less difficult to deal with. In fact, in severe cases of poor mental health it can be far more debilitating and dangerous than a broken leg if it continues for extended periods of time. Having poor mental health does not mean that you are weak, it means you are in need of treatment and support.

Many people have functional levels of poor mental health which can mean they are able to go to work and survive, but other aspects of their life or relationships are negatively impacted as a result. Maybe you hold it together at work, but when you get home you sleep or flop onto the couch, completely drained. Or perhaps, at home you are functional but at work it becomes obvious that something is not quite right.

Most men are poor at talking about their mental health; this is perhaps one of the reasons why the number of men that die by suicide is so high. Trying to abide by gender stereotypes and biases is incredibly damaging, especially if you are trying to fit into a mould that is not you.

We often do not talk about our emotions or feelings and instead clam up and keep everything inside. Talking can help to get some of this off of your chest, exercise can help to funnel some of that stress away, but ultimately the root cause needs addressing instead of ignoring.

There will be instances where medication is more appropriate than therapy, even as a stop-gap intervention, this all depends upon the condition and what you are experiencing. With the wait time for Cognitive Behavioural Therapy in the UK at around two years, medication may be needed during this waiting period to stabilise how you feel. Two years is a long time to wait on the NHS for therapy, many decide to go privately due to the length of time required to wait. When the wait is up you often only get six sessions on the NHS, for many this may not be enough.

Just remember, if you are going through a particularly difficult time there is no shame in asking for help. Around two out of five GP appointments are for people struggling with their mental health (Naylor, 2020); perhaps even higher. It is completely normal to go through difficult times, just make sure you know to seek help when things are too much. There are charities such as MIND and Samaritans that are available for people on the brink of making a permanent decision. We are more likely to make a strong emotional decision when our mental health is poor; this can look different in everybody but if you think people are struggling then letting them know you are there to talk to can make all the difference. Offering to hang out, go for a walk, have a cup of tea or cooking them dinner might be the gesture they need. If you are feeling this way, it may be the gesture you need.

People are more likely to open up if they know you have also struggled, as for me I feel as if they are less likely to judge you and more likely to understand what you are going through. Far more of us struggle or have struggled than you know. Just because you don't see someone walking round with a big "I'm not OK" sticker on their face doesn't mean they are coping.
The last time I talked to a doctor about my mental health guess what? Their mental health was also struggling as a result of the pandemic! They had a wealth of resources available as they had used them themselves to take care of their mental wellbeing. You are not alone, just make sure you talk to those around you and take positive action to try and change your circumstances.

Drugs and alcohol are not the answer; they will make you feel much worse in the long run. If you are not willing and ready to change your negative behaviours, you may end up losing those around you until you are a better person to be around. You have to be willing to make the changes necessary to tackle poor mental health – something much easier said than done.

Our mental health will have ups and downs throughout life, a stress management and resilience course I attended recently talked about how we all have 'cups' with a limited capacity, as different stresses in our life build up and add to this we can become overwhelmed. When this goes on for long periods of time it can cause long lasting symptoms that require medical input to resolve. If you can manage the stresses when they are smaller, you can make sure you are looking after yourself much better in the long term. If you have suffered from burnout it can take a few weeks to years for a full recovery, depending upon the severity.

If you tackle a problem when it is smaller or has just started, you are able to potentially resolve it before it continues to cause negative feelings or thoughts. Life is always going to throw difficult situations and stress our way, if we can learn to better control how we respond to the stress or situation we can develop our resilience. We'll get onto resilience in the next chapter, along with methods of building it.

Knowing when to say no is an incredibly powerful tool to have at your disposal. If you are unable to say no others will continue to take, or to add pressure and workload to you. We have a limited capacity and amount of time to do things in, saying no shows how valuable your time is and can protect you from stress at the same time.

As somebody who has experienced really poor mental health and depression, it is a topic I could talk about for hours. The best advice I can give to you is that if you are struggling and feel like you have nobody to talk to, reach out to a medical professional. We can't solve all of our problems alone, especially when it comes to our mental health. There is no shame in admitting that you cannot do everything by yourself, we are a social species and shouldn't have to try to fix everything without support.

We need to normalise looking after our mental health. Just because we cannot see it as easily each day as a physical injury, the physical symptoms that poor mental health can cause can be far more debilitating than something you can easily see.

This book isn't going to solve all of your problems. It is here as a starting point to get you thinking differently and to try moving out of your comfort zone. The reality is that if you are clinically depressed, stressed or suffering from anxiety, you are going to need much more help than a book can give you.

If you are in a bad place then please speak to someone, you are not as alone as you feel. It is easy to have tunnel vision when you are feeling emotional and unable to see past the fog in your mind, or the emotions that you are feeling right now. This doesn't have to be forever, and there are ways to move through it all and come out the other side stronger than you imaged you could ever be. By talking to someone else you can begin to get more opinions and to build a more objective view, challenging negative thinking patterns and stop the spiralling.

Not everybody reading this will have poor mental health, but many of you reading may be unhappy. It's important to understand that feeling unhappy doesn't mean you have depression or poor mental health. It may be that the life you are currently living is causing you unhappiness or stress.

When this becomes chronic rather than acute (it lasts a long time rather than just feeling unhappy in a particular situation), it may be time to seek some help from a medical professional, such as a doctor for appropriate sign-posting or medication. If you have been unhappy for a few weeks and there is no sign of improvement, speak to somebody. Early intervention can help to start trying to fix the issue, rather than ignoring how you feel and it having a much larger impact on your life.

Our brains are designed to try and protect us from harm, we feel pain when a pin pricks our finger or we hold our hand above a flame to protect us, we feel emotions and negative thoughts in a similar manner; as a defence mechanism.

An emotional response is there to protect us, many of the negative thoughts are responses we have to try and keep us safe. The issue is in the modern world we do not have the same predators and threats we had 500 years ago; there are no wolves, bears or tigers trying to kill us day-to-day, our threats and perceived dangers now are stresses and situations which makes our brains feel uncomfortable.

Our brain is still trying to protect us, but by doing so it can have some extremely negative thoughts; ones which can result in self loathing or thinking of the worst possible scenario. Your mind perceives these as a threat, but you can still tell your brain no, you can tell your brain that it is being silly or irrational and keep it in line. Your brain is an organ, much like your heart, lungs, skin or liver, it is really important to acknowledge that you are not your brain.

The thoughts that you have are your thoughts, but when you are having negative thoughts this is a defence mechanism your brain has been taught to do for thousands of years to ensure humans continue to exist, but this does not mean you are your brain. You can challenge those negative thoughts and frame them differently.

One exercise for deciding if you are thinking emotionally or rationally, is for you to write down how you feel; you can look at this another day and decide how rational you were thinking at the time. As you start to build up an emotional diary you will begin to see trends: what made you feel this way, were your thoughts rational, when you feel that way how do you react? Was your brain going into survival mode and thinking the most negative and painful thoughts to try and protect you from danger? As you start to practice identifying these defence mechanism thoughts, you will start to understand yourself better.

By writing down how you are feeling, or looking at a situation after it has happened, you can begin to build a more rational and objective picture. Try writing down not just negative, but also positive situations and thoughts; we are a sucker for missing the things that are going well and only focusing on the negatives. Focus on the positives too; you will naturally become better at identifying them if you actively try to find the things that went well and the positive thoughts that you have had, not just the negatives.

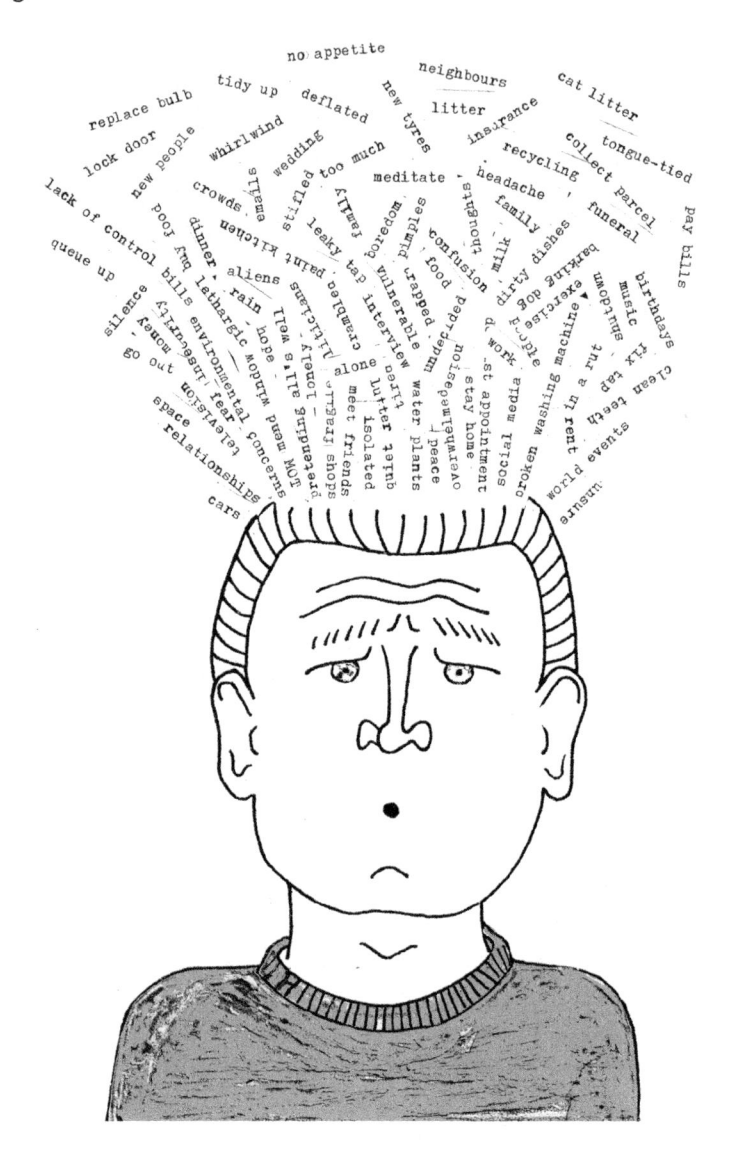

By practicing gratitude and looking for the positives you have had each day, you can begin to make yourself feel happier and increase your wellbeing. Positive psychology is a growing field, and initial studies and tests point to people becoming happier, sometimes dramatically so, in a short space of time by practicing "Three Good Things". Martin Seligman is one of my favourite psychologists; he focuses on flourishing, wellbeing and positive psychology. He is an absolute don in the field, coming up with multiple theories on wellbeing and happiness that are applied and used today by many. He came up with "Three Good things", which is a simple as it sounds.

Think of and write down three good things that happened to you today, and why these happened to you, it is important to write them down to be able to look back on them. They can be as big or as small as you like, the event doesn't have to be life changing to change your life it seems, or to boost your wellbeing, anyway.

Seligman (2011) discovered that by having people focus on their character strengths, as well as practicing looking for the positives each day, some people suffering from depression went from severely depressed to mildly in just a few weeks. The only issue is that these benefits only continued so long as positive psychology was practiced, much like going to the gym and exercising, the benefits were lost over time when not continued. Building healthy psychological habits into our daily routine and life are important to maintain a healthy mind. Much like our physical health our mental health needs regular conditioning to maintain our wellbeing.

We can all have negative thoughts, but being able to challenge them is important. How rational is my brain being, is it having a negative thought to try and protect me from a perceived threat? Am I starting to have a negative spiral? One negative thought to another until you are mentally berating, thinking or even speaking badly of yourself.

Something I like to do when my brain is having a negative

thought spiral, is tell it "no". I challenge it, if I have a negative thought such as "they hate you" or "you didn't do that right" I try to shut the noise down. If you tell yourself out loud to stop thinking like that or to be quiet, or to stop, notice what happens. Try it for yourself next time you are having negative thoughts.

If I am getting angry or agitated I do the same thing, I tell myself it is okay and does not matter that much, because honestly, it usually doesn't.
If the situation will not have long term effects on your life, and is only an inconvenience, then try framing it in a more positive light. If you slip into a victim mentality asking yourself why it always happens to you, you have shifted your perception to a negative one and will perceive other things that happen in a negative light.

Stop being the victim and start making positive changes, negative thoughts can be stopped with positive action. You just have to want it bad enough. You are responsible for your own happiness and wellbeing, the sooner you acknowledge it the sooner you realise you have the power to change your life for better or for worse.

Chapter 6

Accepting Your Flaws and Setting Boundaries

Before you can begin to build and develop yourself, being able to accept all of your flaws and acknowledge they are present is important. Acceptance before change helps to motivate you to make the changes needed to grow as a person. Our flaws are just one part of what makes us who we are, we all have certain traits that many would say are negatives or things we should work on. The reality is that some of these are so deeply ingrained in us that they are part of who we are, if you can use them as a strength, rather than perceiving it as a weakness it's something that can benefit you. You just have to figure out how to use it to your advantage, self-awareness is a powerful tool once you know how to use it.

The easiest way to do this is to connect with others with this 'flaw' or difference, this can be a point of connection and common-ground, rather than something that you hide away and are ashamed of.

For each of us this will be something different, the secret is to accept the flaw as a piece of you; rather than hiding it and being ashamed. That's not to say it isn't something you want to change, but being self-aware can help you to use it to either work for you, or to work on managing it better than you have been.

I'll use myself as an example; I talk a lot, especially when excited, I flit between different topics of conversation and enjoy speaking about my areas of interest. I often don't explore a topic for a long period of time, usually more intense bursts with my attention span finally getting the better of me. This has been true for jobs and work, my CV is all over the place. I often become bored and want a change of scene; as soon as a honeymoon phase of a new job is over I quickly begin to feel trapped and in search of mental stimulation, often leave a job for something new and shiny.

I suspect on some level I have ADHD, but for now that's just what friends and colleagues think until that diagnosis finally goes through. Does this have to be a negative? Absolutely not!

If I embrace this it's something I can use to my advantage, I know I struggle with my attention span and I work best in short bursts; rather than epic slogs and long sessions. By being self-aware of talking a lot, I can reign myself in a little to listen more. Or try to; it's a work in progress, I'll admit. Also, by turning things into a game or a challenge I can use my competitive nature (I hate losing or performing badly) to my advantage.

For work this has meant trying to find an organisation and role that is constantly changing and never the same. Getting stuck in the same repetitive type of work and working on the same projects quickly becomes boring. By teaching others, I have been able to watch them develop and enable for them to grow. This has been interesting and allowed for me to deploy learning theories, and to see first-hand how we all learn differently. However, I still become bored and this is why I am now pursuing a career in the field of psychology and mental health. Perhaps to understand not only others but myself better, whilst providing value and care to those that need it.

The advantage of understanding myself is that I can use the knowledge that I talk lots and have short burst of high energy to quickly and effectively create content about a topic I enjoy. Interested in fitness? Great, I can write, talk or record content on that with a good level of knowledge. Crypto and investing? Also something I'm passionate about! A new or interesting topic? Sure I can research that easily! This has meant blog posts, Youtube videos and podcasts have been mediums that all work for me; so long as the attention and focus can continue.

Gamifying my life is something that helps me to be more productive. Whilst I'm writing this book I use the words typed to spur me on. Can I type another 1,000 words today; am I able to edge closer to my target word count? I have a mental number in my head I want to reach and seeing the numbers slowly increasing over time has helped me to consistently come back to this book. The same for the editing process, as I sit here slaving away trying to craft something I am proud of. By getting one page closer to completion, I feel a sense of accomplishment as I go.

When I am trying to save up I treat it like a game, can I build up enough money to reach my target? Even looking after my health and fitness these short-term goals help to keep me interested by challenging myself, when I would otherwise become bored and lose interest. For work, if I can make it into a game somehow it becomes much more interesting. This may be setting targets or numbers I wish to achieve, or to help others achieve.

If you are aware of 'flaws' or personality traits that you possess, by learning more about yourself you can help to use these to your advantage by harnessing them. Equally, you are able to connect with others over these points. I'm sure I have a lot in common with those who have been diagnosed with ADHD, meaning if I were to talk about that type of content and the strategies I use to work through trying to be productive (trying being the keyword here), people are more likely to connect over those perceived 'flaws'. Especially if this is something you are trying to change, this may help you to realise you are not the only one out there trying to do the same.

Try thinking about yourself and points or qualities that other may see as flaws. Perhaps you are camera shy or shy in person, but this has enabled you to develop your writing skills to a high level. Maybe you could even write a book yourself? What I am trying to say is by being self aware; you can use these to your advantage, instead of them just being a negative, perhaps you will be able to use them to your strength.

There will be certain things you may have to come to terms with about yourself, certain flaws that actually.. aren't so great. These are the changes worth making. We all have the opportunity to be a better version of ourselves, even changing small aspects of ourselves can lead to a completely new version over time. Small changes that stick are better than big ones that don't, sometimes we need a reason to start this change. It may be a life event that humbles us, a negative event that makes us see the error of our ways, or a positive experience that spurs you on.

To be clear, if you are a bit of a dick to people because you can be, this isn't a character flaw. It's just you being a dick. This chapter isn't an excuse for you to be nasty to people, it's accepting who you are right now before you start to acknowledge that aspects of you may be hindering, instead of helping you, to move forwards.

Instead of beating yourself up and being hard on yourself, use the strengths that you do possess already and change the things you want to. Don't worry about fitting in, once you learn to be yourself you will naturally attract people who are drawn to you for who you are. By comparing yourself to other people and others comparing you against the rest of the world you can quickly fall into the comparison trap.

Be a better version of yourself, not another version of someone else.

Once you learn to not care so much about the opinion of others, you will learn to develop a level of self-confidence and self-assurance that will help you to become more comfortable within your own skin. If others are saying negative things and you are accepting and internalising those too, you are facing negativity from both outside and within yourself.

Try to turn down the outside noise; we spend far too much time caring about what other people think about us. If these people aren't even a significant or important part of your life, what does it matter? If they are a significant part of it, then it's your life, you get to live it the way you want to. If you want to live your life the way somebody else wants you to, you may as well be a second version of them. That makes no fucking sense, so take control of your life choices and think kinder of your own existence.

Your body is aware of how you think and feel about yourself, this is why it is incredibly important that you are kind when you talk about yourself. By talking negatively about yourself and putting yourself down you reinforce the negativity and you will begin to believe it more and more, even if you are joking. We are able to escape the negative comments of others by changing our proximity, but we can never escape from our own mind. The ability to talk and think about yourself positively is something you will need to practice throughout life.

Do you think your body can tell the difference between when you are jokingly putting yourself down and when you are actually putting yourself down? By saying it, you make it more real. Be careful with your words, they do have power and can influence how you perceive yourself. By being kinder to yourself and speaking nicer, you can help to improve self esteem, reduce anxiety and to promote your general wellbeing.

In much the same way, positive affirmations can have a beneficial effect. I'm not talking about meditation and speaking to yourself in the mirror necessarily. Sometimes it's just reminding yourself out loud that you have got this and it's going to be OK. If nobody else is giving you positive affirmations, then do it your fucking self. You're fucking great; don't let anyone tell you otherwise. We all have good and bad days, pick yourself up both mentally and physically, tell yourself you can do it and the chances are you'll give it a bloody good shot.

I'm not saying you will always win, but if you don't at least try to win you're setting yourself up for failure before you have even begun.

Boundaries

I would also like to talk about boundaries within this chapter. Boundaries for yourself are important, when to say no, when to stand up for yourself because your values, ideals and self-worth are more important than letting others walk all over you. Another person's liberties end where yours begin; allowing another person to trample over yours shows how little self respect you have for yourself. Standing up for yourself is important, but first you have to believe that it is important. You have to believe that you deserve to be treated well and given a certain level of respect.

I'm of the belief that respect is given but trust is earned, but that is no reason to be nasty to somebody. If somebody is nasty to you for seemingly no reason, you do not have to tolerate this. Even if there is good reason for it, you still don't have to tolerate it.

You are responsible for your own happiness; therefore you are responsible for your own unhappiness too. There is likely a reason for their behaviour, but that justification doesn't suddenly mean it is OK to treat people like shit. It doesn't mean because they are having a bad day that you have to tolerate outbursts or dickhead attitude, and if you happen to be the one reading this that is exhibiting those behaviours, then others do not have to tolerate you either.

If you are able to look past the random outbursts of strangers then all the power to you, by practicing 'not giving a fuck about what strangers say', you'll be much happier overall. Life has all sorts of little stresses, and outbursts can happen to the best of us.

You don't have to be an arsehole, what you say and how you approach boundary setting conversations are important. There is an elegant way and a non-elegant way, depending upon my mood and how tolerant I am feeling people will see one or the other. Reserve your energy and limited fucks for something more important than other people's behaviour you cannot control.

Family, friends, colleagues, whoever it is being a dick I will distance myself from them and seek less and less interaction with that person. I also like to communicate and make clear that I will not tolerate or suffer this behaviour. Why should I? Why should you? We all have disagreements and clashes of values, but there are ways to talk respectfully. It's as much what you say as how you say it. Sometimes, you need to let emotions settle before having a mature conversation.

Setting healthy boundaries in life is vital to ensure you are respecting your own personal needs.
Boundaries can look different to everybody, it all depends upon what you are happy and unhappy tolerating. You get to decide.

This has meant learning to value myself, and respecting those boundaries by setting them and being consistent around the behaviour I will and will not tolerate. If somebody is rude to me, they immediately lose positive interaction from me and I tend to stop listening to them. If they are particularly rude I will end the conversation there and then, often letting the person know they have pissed me off and that I will not be spoken to like that, then leave. It's not about trying to start an argument or finish one, it's about integrity and saying 'I am not OK with this, therefore I am off. Bye.'

I feel as if I have become less tolerant to others' negative behaviour over the years and more likely to speak out and say what I think when in a situation I may have otherwise kept quiet in when younger, probably a confidence thing, or perhaps caring less about what they think and more about how they are making me feel.

You do not have to be malicious or nasty back; in fact I encourage you not to be. I find I tend to distance myself from that person more and more if the behaviour continues and there is no attempt from them to change or have an adult conversation; which is great for cutting out the arseholes in your life. After all, they are doing you a favour by showing how they treat you. When they treat or speak to you badly, it's an opportunity to be like "OK, fine. You saved me the time and energy; you're not somebody I want in my life". They have saved you time by showing how little respect they have for you, much better to accept this and move on. This is trickier with family than friends and easier with lovers than colleagues but it is important to set boundaries and communicate those boundaries so they can be respected.

When you find that somebody is not respecting boundaries, communicate it. If it continues again and again then take that as a sign; they just don't care about them, and by that extension they do not care about you, not really. Take the hint and distance yourself, have more self respect for you.

Chapter 7

Strengthening Your Mental Walls: Resilience and Perspective

Resilience is loosely the ability to still function when difficult situations strike, you will still feel emotions such as anger, frustration or grief, but you are able to better deal with the challenges presented; rather than shutting down or having to escape from the situation altogether.

The lack of control can be a helpless feeling, when there doesn't feel like a way out and all you can feel are the emotions caused by the stress. We tunnel vision easily in life, focusing on one outcome or one goal. It's important to remember that very often life does not go our way, so trying to plan everything out like some perfect master plan isn't going to work. There's nothing wrong with having a destination, but you have to enjoy the journey there too. There will be bumps, but those bumps are an important part of life. They help us become better prepared; they are the character building traits that help to strengthen our resilience and to expand our comfort zone, allowing for growth.

Building mental resilience and changing your perspective to a more realistic positive approach is only going to serve you in a positive manner. You are always going to encounter difficult situations in life and have to face the many stresses that it presents. By increasing your resilience and changing your perspective you can better prepare yourself for all the challenging situations in life.

By having a more realistic approach to life, you can plan for potential pitfalls along the way, as well as hoping for the best outcome. If you are able to adapt and have a backup plan, the chances are you will cope better with adverse situations or stressful environments, where you may have to think quickly and have a solution at hand ready to go. Somebody who is much better at adapting to when a situation does not go their way has already come up with a backup idea. If the plans falls through and they have the self-confidence to make a decision, instead of worrying about the negatives, they will be far better equipped at dealing with tough situations when compared to someone who only has plan A and struggles with change.

Imagine we all have 'containers' of a finite size. Everyone's container is a different size depending upon how resilient we are and what we are capable of dealing with. We all have a certain level of stress occurring, usually from the daily things that we have to deal with. Maybe you didn't get a lot of sleep last night, and then on top of that you skipped breakfast as you overslept and snoozed your alarm a few too many times. Then on your way to work two cars pulled out on you, as you rushed to make it there on time, by the time you have gotten to work you are already feeling the stress, then on top of that everything starts to go 'wrong' that day. People come to you with their problems and you are not feeling grounded enough to come up with solutions to those problems. You feel your pulse quicken and sweat bead down your forehead as you start to feel overwhelmed.

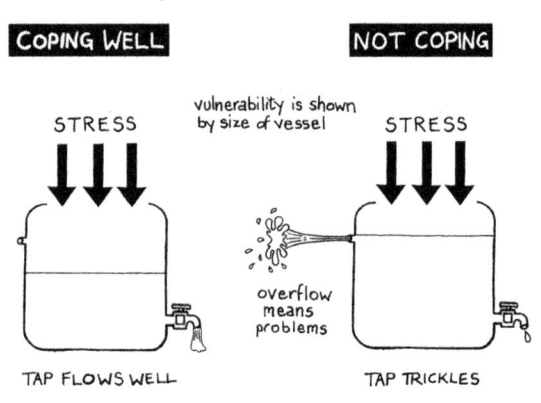

COPING WELL   **NOT COPING**

STRESS   vulnerability is shown by size of vessel   STRESS

overflow means problems

TAP FLOWS WELL   TAP TRICKLES

On top of this there could be larger issues going on in your life that you are thinking about. These often come from stresses relating to work, finances, family or relationships.

The stress can start to escape over the edge, whatever is inside your container will spill out; sometimes onto others. When this happens for a prolonged period of time, our mental health can be negatively impacted, resulting in more difficult to deal with feelings or symptoms that may become chronic. Rather than having a rational response to a situation you may start to exhibit what others perceive as irrational behaviour. Your response to a situation may be more dramatic as you are not capable of rationally dealing with the situation at hand, this could show as anger, sadness or an outburst due to there being more stresses than you can deal with.

This is breaking point. When people are having emotional outbursts such as this their stress containers are too full; their concentration can be disturbed, they make poor judgement and they may even act differently, becoming upset, angry or acting out of character.

Anxiety and excitement are akin to one another; they both cause almost identical physiological symptoms that present in the same or similar way, such as an elevated heart rate, muscle tension, feelings of butterflies, shaking, excessive sweating, and nervousness. However, their cause is different; one is the result of joy and the other from fear. This is because when the nervous system is stimulated a fight-or-flight response is triggered; the amygdala is responsible for both of these emotional responses and so when stimulated can cause similar effects throughout the body.

When we experience amygdala hijack, our brain reacts to psychological stress as if it's physical danger. This is when the fight or flight response kicks in unnecessarily, disabling rational thought or response and is often an overreaction response to stress.

Stress is the body's reaction to a threat, whilst anxiety is the body's reaction to stress. Anxiety can also occur with no obvious trigger, stress is not essential for anxiety to occur, but is often present in the form of amygdala hijack, where the perceived threat is much greater than it would otherwise objectively appear. During a "hijack" the frontal lobes (your logic centres where rational thought occurs) are unable to override it with a more rational response.

Stress is often triggered due to an external event, whilst anxiety can be triggered by thoughts and psychological interpretation of a situation or event.

Long bouts of stress can lead to clinical anxiety, defined as periods of stress that occurs for more than 6 months. This is known as generalized anxiety disorder, where you feel anxious about all events rather than one specific situation. When suffering from chronic stress amygdala hijack can become more frequent, as it increases your levels of fear (Ressler, 2010).

The important thing to realise is that if we take on too much or have too many aspects of our lives challenging us at once, it may be more than you can take. For that reason, becoming more resilient and increasing the size of your container can be a brilliant way to help you to better deal with these stresses, which will inevitably come your way throughout life.

If your container is operating at less than eighty percent then you have the capacity to expand that to one-hundred percent. If you are running at full capacity, then how do you expect yourself to work above your limit? This is where stress and burnout lie; working beyond your means for an extended period of time can have some serious negative effects.

The more stressed you are, the less rationally you are able to think. By reducing some of your stresses you will be able to come up with more effective solutions to problems much quicker. If you are bogged down my multiple stresses then you will being to tunnel vision and struggle to come up with effective solutions to problems. You can also begin to be effected emotionally, which may look slightly different between men, women, and individuals.

How you go about becoming more resilient can look different for each person, it will involve increasing your comfort zone to some extent. However, it can have a negative effect if you try to do too much too soon.

There are a few ways that you can improve your resilience; a lot of the general health advice given to us is actually great for creating a solid base to build from. A good sleep routine, exercise and nutrition will create a better environment for you to flourish, grow and develop your resilience.

There are thought to be 7 Cs within resilience, as proposed by Dr Ginsburg (2016), competence, confidence, connection, character, contribution, coping and control. By building upon each of these aspects he hopes for children aged 18 months to 18 years can learn to build their resilience and coping mechanism. Many of the sample principles can also be applied to adults, to you and me.

A support network is another way to improve your resilience, by creating a solid support system around yourself with friends, family and people to talk to, which will enable you to have people there when you need them. Having more people to spend time with is important, without them you can feel more isolated and this can negatively impact your mental health and end up becoming a stress in your life. By building a support network, you create a social surrounding that also acts as a means to develop your resilience; as well as the previously discussed benefits to hormone release, such as oxytocin from social connections.

Having the ability to reach out is incredibly important, we are not able to deal with all of the stresses of life, nor should we try to. Share the load and the burden, resilience is not about tackling everything on your own, but by having the means to deal with adversity and knowing when to ask for support.

If you are better able to understand yourself, this will help you to determine how resilient you are currently, if you are dealing with too many stresses, these can weigh you down. A stress for one person may not be a stress for another, or it could be a stress for both people but much more stressful for one person than the other. As you begin to understand your limits and areas you are resilient in, you will find it much easier to know when to say "No". You will begin to understand what is too much and what is within your capacity.

Resilience is often related to mental stresses, rather than physical. Some of the stresses that your body experiences can be positive ones like exercise (when correctly balanced with rest), which can have some brilliant effects on your mood, fitness and overall health. The hormones that are released as a result of exercise can help to better regulate cortisol levels, which are responsible for our stress response. You will, however, feel tired and exhausted immediately after exercise. The same is true whilst your body recovers, but there are many positives to exercise when compared to the other types of stress your body can face.

Improving your resilience as a whole is not as straightforward as many of us would like, expanding our comfort zone is one method. Practicing things we enjoy and that give us satisfaction, trying to look after our bodies by getting enough exercise, a diet balanced in macro and micronutrients, enough sleep for our bodies and to reduce our daily stress levels. Other methods of relaxation can help, such as meditation, yoga, going for a walk, swimming, playing an instrument, gardening or playing a sport. Whatever it is that you enjoy that allows for you to switch off a little mentally.

Thought patterns are also an important aspect of this, mind is just one of the factors relating to resilience. Positive affirmations or positive self-talk, particularly in the morning, can be beneficial to start your day off and reinforce the positivity that you need right now. You will know what to say; by saying this regularly you can make it real as you start to believe it more and more. If you are struggling with suggestions, I like to tell myself 'I can do this' or one of my friend's favourites, 'I am a lion'.

Positive thinking can also help to alter your mindset over time, once you accept situations for what they are. Rather than the victim mindset such as 'Why is it always me?', instead a more objective 'OK, this is outside of my control but I can control my reaction to the situation'. Try catching yourself next time you have a negative thought or you are in a negative spiral, is there a more positive way you can reframe it? Challenge the negative thoughts when you have them, is it a rational thought or irrational?

There is nothing wrong with having a negative thought if it really is rational and due, the issue begins when you are having negative thoughts about yourself and those around you regularly. As you learn to be kinder to yourself, you can begin to be kinder to others too as you will have the capacity to do this. The right words can harm, but the same words in a more positive manner can help to build up resilience in yourself and others. It is not just the words you say, but the way that you speak that is important. Tone, body language, facial expressions and pitch of voice all play into how people perceive the message you are giving them. Speaking to yourself is no different.

As you can tell, I love a little exercise, so here goes. First up, draw your container, that big vat of emotional capacity. Now fill it, fill it with all those bloody stresses that you have in your life. The big ones, the little ones, the ones in the back of your mind, write them all down. I like to size them depending on how big of a pain in the arse they are to my day-to-day. Done? You have just identified your current stresses by doing this little exercise.

Next up you want to figure out some solutions to these pesky stresses, start with the easy ones and work up to the more difficult to solve stresses. Didn't sleep well last night? Try sleeping a little earlier tonight. Did you start your day hungry?

Plan to have a snack available to take with you, or prepare breakfast the night before. Make the life of future you easier, instead of problems, hunger and a hangry temper; make smoother sailing for you tomorrow. Treat your future self like a friend, be thoughtful not foolish, get the sleep, make future you happier. Take responsibility for your own shitty decisions and make better ones instead.

Worried about what you are going to buy your aunt Susan for her birthday because she hated last year's present? Fuck it. Who cares? Well obviously Susan, but fuck Susan. She doesn't sound like the best aunt anyway. All I am trying to illustrate here is that don't let the Susan's in your life get to you; there will be many, and their opinions and judgements don't have to be things that add to your already filled stress container.

Is the looming threat of being evicted from your house hanging over your head? OK, that one isn't so simple. Those kinds of stresses are very real and need much more thought and brainstorming to resolve. There is not always an easy fix, that's what I'm trying to illustrate here, but the problems that have an easy solution? Get them gone; make your life an easier and more stress-free one.

You can only handle so much stress before it gets to you, so you are going to have to resolve some of them; usually the easy ones first, the others may have to stay for the moment.

Stress is no joke; I let work become stressful for me and had to take a step back, so I could get a handle on both work and my personal life for six months. There is no shame in this, things are fine now but it took a trip to the GP and making changes to my life to manage this. For your own benefit, get a grasp of those stresses before they get a grasp of you first. You can only care about so many things before it becomes too much for you, when you stop caring about the less important, it is such a liberating feeling. Not to say that you don't care, but accepting you can only influence a limited number of things; your own actions and reactions.

I discovered that so many things don't matter to me, that single realisation was perhaps one of the biggest for me in terms of becoming happier. If there aren't as many things causing me stress, then I'm not going to be as stressed. Not to sound like Captain Obvious but the less you care about the bullshit in life, the more you will be able to care about the things you do give a fuck about.

If there is a limited capacity that we have to work to, take things out. Less is more, or less is less but it gives you the capacity to care more about the right things. Next time something small gets to you, try letting it go. Does it even really matter that much? If it's not going to ruin your life, don't let it ruin your day. We all care about different things; something that you care about someone else might not, so let's just make it clear that just because you don't care about it doesn't mean other people don't. That's the fun thing about life, none of us are the same and it would be so bloody boring if we were. We all value different things, they may be important to you and not to somebody else, or vice versa.

By being able to adopt a positive, realistic but optimistic approach and view to life you will begin to feel happier overall. A glass half full or a glass half empty approach is all about perspective, perspective is important as this is how you frame things in your mind. One thing you can change is how you view a situation. I'm not asking you to pretend everything is perfect, being overly positive can come back to bite you; life is not perfect and things do not always go well, in fact life is fucked and often times we have to just accept we don't always have the answers to fix it. However, if you can change, or begin to change, the way that you think, the way that you perceive things and how you view them, this can begin to have a positive effect on others around you.

Your reactions and use of language is more likely to be positive, you're more likely to smile at a stranger or to say hello. You're more likely to give a fuck, to be able to give a fuck, to have that capacity, to want to. Change starts with you; resilience is about how **you** are able to cope with situations and in turn how you react to them, depending upon your perspective and capacity at the time.

If you can bolster your resilience levels, you'll become a formidable person, capable of dealing with challenging situations and making better on-the-stop decisions. Resilience can take a long time and a lot of work to improve, but it feels brilliant when you manage to.

Chapter 8

Creative Outlets & Reflection

Creativity is often undervalued as a tool, when was the last time you took a moment to create? Self-expression might seem like a distraction, but it can be used as a method for reflection and downtime that we desperately need. It can be used as a means to distance yourself from your worries, to allow for reflection or as an outlet for you to create something that expresses how you are feeling. As an added benefit, it can also boost your resilience when used as quiet time.

The fast-paced living of the modern day means that a lot of people often do not allow for time to reflect. Instead, deciding to distract themselves from the present, rather than reflecting and making sense of a situation or emotions being felt. Allowing time to process, however that may look, is important. If you push it down without processing it can come back and negatively influence how you feel later on in your life. Don't run from your problems and issues; there is no growth in that, just avoidance and stagnation.

You have your typical types of creative activities; drawing, painting, singing, music. Things defined as "the arts" but there are so many forms of creativity. From writing, photography, designing clothing, graphic design, hairdressing, knitting, pottery, dancing, yoga, martial arts, cooking, making videos about something you love or enjoy. There really are many forms of creativity in the modern world, and sometimes picking a form that you enjoy as either a means of downtime, or to help you express, can be a valuable investment of time.

The key is to give things a try, by creating something rather than consuming you are able to literally bring something into the world that nobody else can (or at least not the exact same way you did). There is also a sense of achievement when you successfully make or create; you baked a cake that tastes amazing? Congratulations, you just expressed yourself! As cheesy as it sounds, there is some truth to this.

Try different things, give them a go and find an activity that allows you to express yourself, if it's through creative flare or just a way for you to unwind and relax. You'll feel a lot better for giving yourself time to do what you want.

Maybe you just want to find something that helps you to unwind, or perhaps you're looking to turn a form of expression into a side hustle. Whatever the situation may be, don't neglect your own creativity. Like I talked about in the earlier section, find your passion by doing. If you aren't willing to try new things or revisit old interests and hobbies then how do you expect to progress? The truth is, it's on your own terms. You are directly responsible for your own self, and if you have been neglecting this, then perhaps it is time that you started to give yourself time to just be you.

If you are spending time creating something, you are spending less mindless time on your phone or on the internet too, you get a dopamine hit because you achieved something by making, not just consuming or watching. There's no guilt if you have actually done something you consider productive, rather than falling victim to the isolation and negative mental health that endlessly scrolling social media can have. It can also allow for a state of flow to occur, if you are engaging in a challenging yet enjoyable activity.

To reflect and unwind you don't have to even have a creative outlet, many people find cleaning or organizing calming.

Certainly not a creative outlet, but it gives them time to switch off and focus on the task at hand. You may already have an activity like this that you use to relax, something that calms you and allows for you to escape reality for a while. This peace and space can help you to reflect upon, well, whatever it is you want to reflect upon. A situation, an experience or a dilemma you have. Quite frankly you can reflect on whatever you want, there aren't any rules.

So, what the hell am I talking about when I say reflection?

You're probably thinking "I already know what reflection is, so what the hell are you on about?" And this may be true, but despite knowing what reflection is, do you sit down and properly reflect after the fact? This type of reflection is called reflection-on-action, where you are reflecting after a specific event or circumstance that has prompted you to think about it. Usually this happens after a negative experience, as we often forget to reflect when something positive happens.

Reflection can be as specific or as broad as you wish to make it, you could be reflecting upon how you feel about a person, a place or an event that occurred. The importance of reflection is that you can essentially take a step back and take an objective view of something, rather than being in the situation where you may make decisions based on strong emotions. You can't see your own reflection in boiling water; let your emotions calm before trying to make a decision.

By practising reflection-on-action and looking back at a situation that has happened, you can learn to begin practising reflecting and how you could have done things differently. Usually people reflect on negative events, but it's incredibly important to reflect on the positives too.

Most people do not have a high level of self-worth. What I mean by this is that a lot of people do not believe deep down they are worthy of praise and compliments. If you have performed particularly well, or someone compliments you, if you do not believe it yourself you will brush off what the other person is saying. How many people do you know that suck at taking compliments? Call someone good looking or say that they look nice and they'll shoot you down immediately, as they don't believe it themselves, so how could anyone else think that of them?

Now, reverse the scenario. Someone has said something negative about you, or put you down in a way. You are much more likely to take this on board and internalise this. If someone is repeatedly told something they will believe it. It is important to tell yourself that you can succeed. Other people are always going to have voices and opinions. **_Try turning the noise off._** If that person wouldn't show up to your funeral, why the hell do you care what they think?

What others think about if you can succeed or not isn't important. If you believe in yourself you are much more likely to succeed, if you don't believe in yourself you have already set yourself up to fail before you begin. It is important to have a level of self awareness and how your language and actions can affect others. I'm not suggesting you tip-toe around others, but if you are finding you seem to piss everyone off all the time, perhaps reflecting upon your current self is important. Do you want to be an arsehole forever? I'm not telling you to second guess your actions constantly, but taking a moment to look back can help to guide you through future experiences, and being less of an ass-hat can have its benefits.

By becoming more self-aware this can also lead you to not only reflect during a situation but have a better awareness of you own use of language, response and better control over your emotions during a difficult conversation. If this is something you are interested in, then learning more about reflection is super easy. There are numerous articles on reflection; with a lot of them being clinical reflection.
For now, that covers some of the basics. Next up let's give

reflection an actual go. Right here, right now. Grab a pen and paper. I always find pen and paper is better than a keyboard, as you are forming the words in your head, it makes them seem a lot more real. Then think of a recent situation that you can reflect on, usually a particularly bad or particularly good one is easiest as they stand out a lot more as a memory, due to the strong emotions that you felt at the time.

With your piece of paper describe the situation as you remember it, how you felt and what you were thinking, and then evaluate the situation, particularly highlighting the good and bad parts. This is an incredibly strong tool to analyse a situation that has already happened, this model is referred to as Gibb's reflective cycle and can be applied in almost any situation or circumstance (Gibbs, 1988).

Analysing the situation is an important step too, what sense can you make of it? How aware were you of different elements? Look to bring elements of Description, Feelings and Evaluation into the Analysis portion, bringing the elements together. After this a conclusion and action plan are important for planning on how you could deal with the situation better if it arose again, or to highlight that everything you could do was already done.

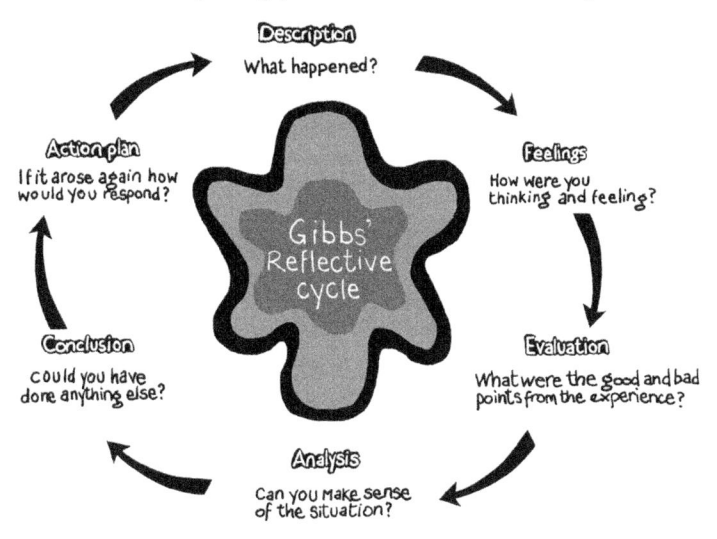

Description
What happened?

Feelings
How were you thinking and feeling?

Evaluation
What were the good and bad points from the experience?

Analysis
Can you make sense of the situation?

Conclusion
Could you have done anything else?

Action plan
If it arose again how would you respond?

Gibbs' Reflective cycle

The aim is to be able to look at a situation, break it down into individual chunks and at the end have a plan of how you would tackle it again if the situation arose once more. You might find that you do this through conversation with a friend sometimes without even realising it, but by actively reflecting with the intent to improve you are only going to better yourself.

By incorporating both reflection and creativity into your life, you should hopefully see positive results. By allowing yourself downtime to express and passively reflect, as well as actively reflect; where you sit down with the intent to look at a specific situation or event.

You can really see benefits to your overall mindset and thought process by practising this. It doesn't take too long to try, if you find it doesn't work for you then you haven't wasted time. Look at it as finding out something new about yourself. Congratulations, you're already taking steps to become more aware about yourself and what methods work for you.

If it does work, well even better – Reflection is an incredibly important method to rationalise a situation and how and why it occurred. If it was a positive situation, it may be reflecting on what went well. If you are trying to replicate this success or positive moment, you can break down and analyse how you can achieve this. If the situation or outcome was negative, you can see where things broke down and how to achieve a different result next time.
I'm going to give you an example of a recent reflection I did myself to help figure out what I want from life, I'm going to break myself down as a person. My wants, needs, likes and dislikes.

I want to make a difference, I know that much. Helping people is something that comes naturally to me. For this reason I've considered the police, the NHS and even the fire brigade. But the insecurity and uncertainty of being a fire officer.. as well as the heights were definitely not for me. Deep down I think I want to be a hero, as crazy and self centred to say that's the truth.

I want to make a difference and also be acknowledged for it, I want my hard work to be seen.

More recently I've considered the police again, my knee and back could be an issue but honestly it's tempting to give it a try. Even if it's to be told that "No" is the answer, something fulfilling with purpose is the current pursuit for me. I know I need variety, but I also need structure. Too much routine I hate, but not enough of a plan or clear targets and I can become distracted and disengaged. When I'm set a task I do it to the best of my ability, but I like to do it quickly. I'm like three people in one, needing freedom, routine, structure, stimulation, variety and achievable challenges, the repetitive is.. repetitive, I enjoy responsibility and making choices, but too much responsibility can feel crushing.

The overall feeling I have is wanting to make a difference, wanting to help, to make things better for people. To provide value and be recognised for that, the self improvements that can happen and the impact that one person can have on you is more than most of us realise. One person can make a difference.

I'd like to make people happy, to help them live a happier life and enable them to bring out their own potential. Guiding others to become happier versions of themselves, to enable them to look after themselves independently and bolster their wellbeing. Whilst doing this, I realise I have a deep desire to be wanted and valued by others. Perhaps craving the external validation from others I struggle to provide internally. This seems like more of an insecurity, I should look to self validate and self value more. Ultimately the opinions of most others are not something I can control or should try to control.

Would being a therapist be something that gave me purpose? Having become a mental health first aider, I decided this type of work is not only fulfilling but enables others to make positive change. This is one of the reasons I decided to pursue a Masters in Psychology, this exercise helped me to discover what is truly important to me and what I want to pursue.

Something else I could have done is to gain experience or shadow to see what these roles truly look like on a day-to-day, when I thought I had an idea of what interested me pursuing that idea further and approaching others who are in the field to gain more information. Having met lots of people working within the mental health world, I knew I got along with them well and their positive outlooks were refreshing. What I don't yet know for sure is exactly what their work looks like each day, so this is something I could not only have done differently but could do right now to gain more insight. We often think we know what people do, but until we really see it we do not truly know.

As an exercise it is a little lengthier than some others, but the value that you can gain from it is obvious. I like to reflect from time to time to ensure I am doing what is right for me and I am staying true to myself. If you find that your current life and career does not align with your values and beliefs, then perhaps it is time to consider a change.

This type of inward reflection is important, it allows for us to take a moment and understand what our motivations and values are. What drives you? If you had to do the same thing over and over again what thing would you choose? What tasks do you often find yourself lost in, within a state of flow as time passes by in a flash? These are important questions we must ask ourselves every once in a while, because when our values and wants detach from our reality we can have an unfulfilled desire or need that is unmet. If you are lacking direction or unsure of what to do next it's a fantastic way to understand yourself better.

We don't need to have all of the answers, especially when you are younger and still tasting the colours of the world. In fact, I find it absurd that society expects eighteen year olds to know what they want and to have their whole career planned out, attending university for a degree that may, or may not even be used. Most people do not know at the young age of eighteen what they want to have for dinner, never mind having their whole future planned out. You may be fortunate enough to know your likes and dislikes by this age, but having hardly scratched the surface of adulthood, many have no idea about their five year plan, let alone their life plan.

Do you know your five year plan right now? Do you right now, hand on heart know your next step? If so, good for you - the next step is the most important step, even if it's not the right one it will inevitably open up opportunities. Better to take action than be frozen by the thought of uncertainty, better to make a choice than no choice, better to leap than end up stuck and unhappy.
As we change throughout life, our wants and needs also change. We may enjoy a different job, different hobbies or become friends with different types of people as we adapt and grow through our lifetime.

Much the same as our taste buds change over time so do our wants and needs. At age 20 you may have very different wants to age 30 and at 35 you may have different wants again; this will continue throughout life. For this reason, making sure you understand what is driving you forward and knowing yourself are vital to make sure your life aligns with you as a person.

Chapter 9

Goal Setting & Positive Habits

Settings goals can be an incredibly powerful tool for motivation in the short-term, especially if you manage to continuously do this to create a sense of achievement and motivation. While this can work as a nice little trick, remember that you will always be more motivated by a deep-seated motivation rather than something that you want to do yourself, just because it's a fleeting urge.

You may want to run a marathon, but why do you want to run a marathon? What is your motivation for this? To raise money for a cause that took a loved one, or because well.. you haven't run one before and want to give it a shot?

The stronger the motivation or emotion to do something, the more likely you are to achieve a goal. So first really evaluate a goal and how likely you are to achieve it before setting it. If it's a fleeting want or thought you will be less likely to see it through. If you are feeling uncomfortable enough, or your 'pain' is great enough a goal is more likely to be met; think pain points here, like in business, rather than literal physical pain. The more you want something the higher the chance you will work towards this goal. Obviously, using your pain or situation to motivate you works well in the short-term, but a longer term reason will have to keep pushing your forward, perhaps a deep want, value or belief of yours.

Are the motivating factors high enough to push you towards completing your set goal? If the obstacles in your path are greater than the perceived rewards you are going to reap, re-assess your path to the goal. The goal may not be a bad fit, but have you added in too many steps to get there making it overly complicated?

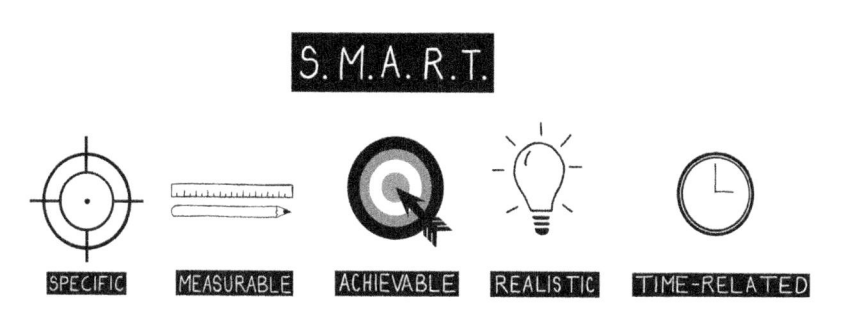

S.M.A.R.T.

| SPECIFIC | MEASURABLE | ACHIEVABLE | REALISTIC | TIME-RELATED |

Keep it simple, stupid (KISS) is a wonderful little acronym if you are making things overly complicated for no reason. If the barriers to your goal are feeling more like a wall, you'll give up before even starting. Remember; keep it simple so you can get started sooner, rather than over-planning for too long. If you keep it simple, you are much more likely to start working towards your goal.

If you can be S.M.A.R.T about your goal setting, the chances of you reaching the end are much higher. Make the goal specific, measurable and achievable. Break it down into bite-size pieces if it's a huge goal, smaller goals are much more manageable. If you're going to eat an orange, you don't usually put the whole thing in your mouth; you eat it piece by piece. This is the same for tackling big tasks; chip away at them piece by piece.

Tackling your goals and making them realistic will do wonders for your motivation, if your motivation is especially low you will find doing a day-to-day list will help you to really focus and achieve too. It could be work related, daily tasks such as washing up, or finally completing that ever elusive task you have been putting off forever. If you give yourself a time-frame this can be helpful too, as you are setting a deadline to when you want to achieve this by.

The key is to make yourself accountable, earlier on I talked about how making yourself accountable to someone else can help. By creating a list, you are making yourself accountable to the list and yourself. Did you manage to do the thing you said you were going to do? If not, how come? Instead of making excuses, try and see why you are not managing to achieve a goal.

Making a list is a nifty little trick, but it does work wonders for most people, even for a short while. Just remember this only helps in the short term; it's not some wonder trick to reach the things that you really want out of life.

Didn't finish a goal or a task that you really want to? Stick it on the next list! By doing this you will see what is important to you by repeatedly writing it down. Let's say you want to work out or go to the gym three times a week, by accomplishing this you will feel a sense of achievement. For each day you miss, figure out why. Do you not want the result enough, or are there other barriers stopping you? Instead of making excuses, start taking actions to allow you to complete your goal.

Here's an example, right now I am setting myself a daily word limit I am aiming to write, on top of this I broke each section down with a rough word count I wanted to achieve. Why? Because it's motivating to ensure this book actually gets finished and not left as another half-completed word document. By creating an overall structure and by breaking it down section by section, it becomes much more achievable mentally. The outcome of the book is no different, but the perceived difficulty is much lower in my mind.

As well as doing this, I am making sure I take a little time away from writing. I'm not forcing myself or punishing myself when I don't manage to write, as all I will achieve is making myself unhappy by punishing myself. Instead, I write when I feel like it, and listen and read the work of other authors in downtime to take inspiration from them and to challenge some of my own ways of thinking.

Personally, I find starting the hardest. Once I am actually doing the thing I set out to do it becomes much easier, try reducing the barrier to getting started so you can chip away at your objective or goal. Action leads to motivation, waiting to become motivated in the hope you will do something is backwards. Do something, even if it is a smaller part of what you need to do, and then the motivation will come afterwards.

Using the gym example, have everything after work ready to go, workout clothes, water bottle and then I'm off. Don't overcomplicate it by bringing changes of clothing, shoes, shower stuff, etc. If you are going to do this, have it all ready to go the day before.

This creates a much higher barrier for myself each day if I don't prepare beforehand and means I would be less likely to workout at all. In fact, a little voice in my head goes "That's too much work, just go tomorrow". I find if I have everything ready to go in the morning, then after work I can just drive over to the gym and do my thing. It's the ***thinking*** about it that gives me time to back out; the ***doing*** is the easy part.

This is only an example; some may find working towards their goal much easier in the morning whilst your brain is fresh. If after work is difficult try making time early in the morning. If you have kids and are limited to certain periods of free time each week or month, then all the more reason to reduce the barriers to your goals.

If you have a big goal you are working towards, setting yourself checkpoints towards the big overall goal will help with the sense of achievement along the way. Splitting the overall goal into bite size tasks you are able to measure will generate a much higher sense of achievement. By making your goal a set of smaller tasks, it makes reaching the end much more realistic. A giant task can seem overwhelming and daunting if you are dreaming big, look at the next step that you need to take instead.

Don't forget to make your goals realistic, if your goals aren't being met look at them and try to figure out why not. Is it a motivational issue, or is your current ability holding you back? Maybe the bar was set a little too high and needs lowering down to begin with? Identify the reason and adjust accordingly so you are able to consistently achieve your set targets.

This does not work for everybody; sometimes just starting is the best way for those that become overwhelmed with the thought of starting. There are all sorts of productivity methods, such as the Pomodoro, consisting of bursts of work with 5 minute breaks, "Eat the frog" where the most difficult task is completed first, and Monk mode where you shut off all distractions for an hour, two hours, or whatever period of time you are aiming for. During this period of time you have to solely focus on the task at hand. I'm not going to sit here and tell you what method is best for you, because I don't know you. You know yourself, so take advantage of that.

Whatever you find works for you, try to make a habit of it and build it into your schedule. The difficult part is identifying what helps you to achieve a more productive routine. We are all different, it is important to acknowledge this as there is no "one size fits all" method for being productive.

"Successful people form habits" this is a quote you will often see thrown around and people trying to give you motivational speeches preaching that this is the case. The truth is, they're not wrong. It takes somewhere between 21 and 66 days to form a habit, or so a quick Google will tell you. So if you are looking to develop yourself further and to form positive habits, you need to put in a little work and a lot of consistency.

It could be something you decide to adopt as part of your

daily routine, perhaps you spend thirty minutes in the morning exercising, or give yourself time to meditate and have some peace and quiet. Whatever it is, the truth is that developing positive habits will enable you to continuously practice something that you find benefiting to you as a human.

It's difficult for me to tell you which habit you should develop, so instead I'll leave a little list here for some of the top habits to help with motivation. You can give each one a try and see what works for you, as we're all different, what works for one person may not always work for another. You will quickly find the methods that do work for you and those methods that you really don't enjoy.

Most of the habits I am about to list are general ones that almost anyone can incorporate into their daily or weekly life. Lifestyle changes that promote health and wellbeing are going to create a better environment for you to succeed and thrive. If you are feeling generally unhappy with life, start by building a few of these into your life. You don't have to do them all at once, it actually feels much more achievable if you pick one and make it part of your routine, rather than turning everything up to 11 at once. The added benefit here is that you will see how each one makes you feel individually, make one change at a time and try to measure the differences you notice. You do have to give the chosen habit a chance, though. Between one and two months is a good length of time, unless you find that you absolutely hate it or it has a negative effect on your health for some reason.

Waking earlier and waking consistently are great habits to adopt. By creating a regular sleeping and waking pattern you can not only plan your day better, you will feel better for it too. This can take a little while to get used to, especially if you have the tendency to stay up late and not get enough sleep. If you can program your body to naturally wake up a little earlier than normal, you can effectively create "more" time, a lot of successful people wake up early, like super early.

5AM or 5.30AM seems to be a pretty common time to start the day off before anyone else is awake. This effectively gives you time in the morning to meditate, exercise, work undisturbed or listen to a podcast that you may not otherwise have had 'time' to do during the day. This will not work for everybody, some people are not good at mornings and you should not force yourself to wake up at this time if it reduces your productivity and has your feeling groggy all day.

Good sleep is more important than waking up at 5AM. You know when you work best and if this is even an option or not. Personally, you won't catch me dead at 5AM. Or more accurately I would be dead if I woke up at that god awful time of day; not for me thank you. If it works for you, all the power to you, but I need a solid eight to nine hours and my idea of fun is not bed at 8PM every night. 10PM, perhaps.

Having space for yourself is important, you can allow for proper space which is healthy for the mind, as well as productivity. By creating a spot in the day that is strictly for things that you want to do, the rest of the day should feel less of a chore. As an added bonus, if you manage to do this in the morning before you start your day, you are effectively ahead of others in terms of productivity and can start your day feeling motivated. I realise this will not be possible for everybody; perhaps you find you are generally more productive in the afternoons or evenings. What is important is that you are carving some time out for yourself. The key point of a regular waking pattern is good quality sleep, to have you waking up and feeling prepared to tackle the world and all of its terrors.

Exercise is perhaps one of my favourite recommendations; it's amazing for not only creating a routine to follow, but it is also brilliant for your mind and body. Humans were designed to move, but the truth is in the modern world a lot of people neglect this. If you are not exercising or eating well, then you are already putting not only your body, but also your mind at a disadvantage.

Incorporating regular exercise into your weekly or daily routine can really help to boost motivation levels; there are all sorts of endorphins that are released when you exercise. It also helps to teach you discipline, you don't get results fast or easily and you have to consistently stick at it to see results. There is a lesson to be learned here. Things that are worthwhile don't come easy, and things that are easy aren't worthwhile. Okay, that's not always true but you get the point. Things worth sticking to are generally not easy, exercise is certainly not easy but the benefits that it can provide you over the years are worthwhile. The added bonus of teaching patience and consistency are an extra along the way.

Meditating is another way to carve out time for yourself to reflect, often thought of as a monk sitting cross-legged underneath a waterfall, as he or she endures the force of nature. Or maybe that's just how I imagine it, kind of a weird image but that's what springs to mind. The truth is that this isn't really the case. Meditation can be as simple as allowing yourself five minutes of peace each day to sit down and relax. This is something I was doing most days without even realising it was meditation to begin with. Sit down, relax and let your mind do the wandering. It's meant to be particularly effective if you write down your thoughts straight after you have finished, but honestly just having some peace can be good to help you reset and just not think about anything.

Creating time for "you" is important, to let you enjoy life and the things that you as a person like to do. Whatever it may be, giving yourself 30 to 60 minutes each day to practice something that you enjoy you can dramatically improve the quality of your life. Instead of watching that Netflix show or TV, try creating some time for something that you genuinely enjoy and is also productive. I'm not saying there is anything wrong with a bit of mindless binging, we all do it and sometimes that's just what we need.

But if you manage to cut down on shitty TV, each day should

feel a little more positive and productive, as you are actively developing a skill or being creative. Maybe not wasting hours watching TV or scrolling through the internet will help you to feel a little better about yourself, as you have more time to do things that you want to.

Creating a daily "To-do" list for the next day can help to organize your thoughts before bed, this should help to make sure it is all written down and doesn't keep you awake at night. It also helps to keep your day structured the following day, meaning you don't waste time trying to remember what you were going to do, or worse yet, forget completely.

An added benefit is that if you are feeling worried or stressed this can also help you to relax; you won't be forgetting anything and the list will be there in the morning to help guide your day. When I have a lot on my mind I like to do this, or I am feeling particularly overwhelmed or stressed over something. I find when something is on paper and not in your head, it gives you a little more room to forget whatever it was you were trying to think about five second ago and not feel worried about it.

Journaling or writing can be a fantastic way to express your emotions and really understand how you feel, by creating time each day to write feelings and thoughts down; you can really break your day down mentally. This is a form of reflection and is incredibly powerful when you are intentional about it. By externalising an emotion or feeling (putting it onto paper, instead of just feeling the emotion) you will find it much easier to analyse. The same reason people are bad at taking their own advice, yet offer brilliant advice to others is that there is not enough reflection going on. As you become more self aware and intentional about how you feel and respond to a situation, you will also find it easier to change your response; if you want to.

We all have times we want to tell someone to fuck off, there is nothing wrong with that either, but if you find yourself doing this to everyone then maybe it's time to change it up. On the flip side, if you are always trying to people please but it's finally time you stand up for yourself maybe today is the day.

Acknowledge your negative or "bad habits", this is really key if you want to start working on dropping the bad ones and starting up some more positive habits. Maybe you're particularly tough on yourself, or you never listen to others. Whatever your bad habits may be, try curbing them as you develop more beneficial ones.

Think big, but start small with your habits. Build up slowly rather than diving in the deep end, you are more likely to stick at something you can manage, rather than something that seems too difficult to stick to. Maybe you're just fine the way you are. Change for the sake of change defeats the purpose of all this, but giving yourself time to question who you are and unpick qualities you would like to change can be really quite beneficial. For me, I'd love to be less jealous when it comes to partners. I know it stems from a deep down insecurity and it something I have been working on overcoming for the past few years; the thing is it really is taking years to get better at. But that's OK, change can be slow. Some of these "bad" habits or qualities can take a long time to change. After all, it's essentially changing who you are.

This is the same for creating routine, achievable changes have longevity, rather than extreme ones that will have you boomeranging before you know it. Some of those changes just will not come naturally at all; if you have tried and tried maybe it's just not supposed to be. I find if I procrastinate and really struggle to do something no matter how many times I try, maybe not caring and giving up is fine too. It just means I don't want it that much and it was a nice thought while it lasted. Sometimes I find that caring less about something I want helps to make it happen.

They say in relationships not to force things, when it's right it will happen and you'll find the right person. You can apply this to all sorts of situations outside of finding your other half. If you try too hard you will become so fixated on every failure and it will hurt that much more when things go wrong. Mix things up and try a different approach, caring less can work for some people. When I care too much about something emotions can become stronger and this throws me off my game, you see this happen in sports a lot when the pressure gets to players.

Slow and steady wins the race when it comes to life. Consistency is key; if you want to achieve a larger goal it will take time and effort. It's important to remember that change is uncomfortable, if you have started to make changes and you find it difficult... "This is what difficult feels like" is an Alex Hormozi quote that I feel is really important to acknowledge. Most of the things worth achieving in life are not easy, in fact, they are difficult. However, once you start to work these difficult changes into your day-to-day life, they start to feel less uncomfortable and difficult.

The important lesson is that it gets easier, the better you get at doing something the less difficult it feels over time. But it's going to feel difficult, almost nothing worth doing is easy and if it was then where is the sense of achievement when you do hit that milestone and achieve what you set out to do?

Do the hard work so that you can enjoy the benefits of it later on, but don't make yourself miserable along the way. The journey is even more important than the destination, happiness is in the journey, the now. You can build a happier life around yourself, but you don't find happiness in the future, you find it in the present. It might be that you have to make some changes along the way to make the present something that you can appreciate and enjoy more.

Chapter 10

Escaping Your Comfort Zone & Expanding Horizons

Everyone is more comfortable in their comfort zone, it's just the truth. It's named as such because there is no risk there; be it financial risk, status risk or risk of a stressful situation. In fact, there is so little risk in your comfort zone you may just become complacent. The comfort zone should be renamed to the stagnant zone, because there is no change or adaptation in this place.

The issue with complacency is growth, how do you grow as a human being if you never push your boundaries or try new things? Perhaps your comfort zone **does** including trying new things, but to really develop yourself as a person and to lead a happier lifestyle you are undoubtedly going to have to leave this zone at some point.

Maybe it includes leaving the financial safety of a job that you are unhappy in, maybe it includes cutting ties with someone who is a big part of your life but is incredibly toxic, or perhaps it is something as simple as meeting new people. Whatever it may be, to step outside of your comfort zone and start growing further as a person is important in life.

There is a saying, "There is no growth in the comfort zone, and no comfort in the growth zone." I couldn't track down exactly who said it for sure, but it's one of those online inspirational quotes that you often see. But if you think about it, it does make sense. If you are actively staying in situations that you are already comfortable with, how can you enhance yourself as a human further?

How will you ever take risks and make it places if you stay where you are and refuse the unknown? The thing with the comfort zone is that it maintains the status quo, things stay the same and this feels safe. The issue with safe is that it doesn't allow you to grow as a person or to improve at things that make you feel uncomfortable.

One of the most common situations where this may be true is social anxiety, obviously if you are suffering from anxiety and being surrounded by large or loud groups triggers a panic attack then perhaps don't go diving head first into situations that send you into terror. But instead perhaps by pushing your comfort zone gently to enter the learning zone you can gradually overcome this fear. Here's a little illustration to help visualize what I mean.

Here there are four zones described, comfort, fear, learning and growth. I would perhaps add a further zone beyond growth, the panic zone. Obviously, panic is ideally avoided; nobody enjoys too much stress, particularly if you are suffering from conditions that exacerbate this.

The size of everyone's comfort zone is different, and what is included or excluded in that zone too. Familiarity is vital, the more you are familiar with a situation the less likely it is to cause you panic or stress. By leaving the comfort of the centre and instead pushing out towards your learning zone you can begin growing and expanding which situations you are comfortable in. It is thought that activities that are deemed valuable by you, you are more likely to try – even if they make you feel anxiety or fear (Kiknadze & Leary., 2021).

Now social anxiety is just one form of discomfort, everyone has certain situations they are uncomfortable with. It could be something as simple as not liking to answer the phone or becoming stressed in a situation you are unfamiliar with. This could be standing up and presenting, appearing on video, engaging in conversation with people you do not know or learning a new skill you have never done before or are not confident in.

While change is scary it leads to personal growth and happiness in the long-run. A fantastic example of this would actually be COVID-19, think of all the change that has had to occur in order for us to adapt. Initially it was quite scary, with a lot of uncertainty but quickly it became the new "norm". Wearing masks into shops and ensuring you regularly wash your hands become nothing but another habit, even scanning into places you spent more than 15 minutes in became somewhat normal.

Now, I'm not attempting to say COVID has made anyone happy, far from it. The point that I'm trying to illustrate is that change and adaptation to a situation that for most of us was quite scary or uncertain, was less scary once we were familiar with it. Humans are scared of the unknown, rather than the situation itself more often than not, that is why so many of us are scared of the dark. It's the unknown, the not seen, where our imagination takes hold.

Take me for example, I hate exams. No matter how much preparation and learning I put into an exam I will still be nervous and anxious. The more exams I have sat the easier and less stressful they have become for me, but even to this day they still give me butterflies. However, over time they have become a lot less scary and while I may not enjoy them, they are something that can be tackled in a much more effective way. The saying "practice makes perfect" isn't one I like, practice makes better and better feels like you are able to muddle through. Sometimes muddling through is all that you need.

What holds us back is usually fear, fear of rejection, disappointment or embarrassment. Perhaps you previously had a bad experience and it put you off a certain situation or activity forever, you end up building something up to be a lot scarier than it actually is. True growth occurs when you can push through that discomfort and fear, you are able to make a breakthrough in personal growth.

There's nothing quite like overcoming a situation that years or even months before you could never imagine yourself tackling. Making an active effort to live outside of your comfort zone will change you as a person for the better. Just remember it won't be easy, you will have failures and that's part of the process. Learn from them, improve from them. That's what we humans do, we learn, adapt and improve to come back better than before.

Once you have acknowledged your dislikes or discomforts, you can really start to take the time to expand your comfort zone to include a situation or activity that perhaps you once hated. If you are bad at something, or at least deem yourself bad at it, you are less likely to actively go out of your way to try improving. With a shift in mindset this can be overcome, try challenging yourself here by trying something new and exciting; something that makes you nervous but doesn't leave you shaking in your boots at the thought of trying it.

Challenge yourself to pick one thing you would like to overcome or become better at. Perhaps it's answering the phone, having the confidence to talk to strangers, learning to swim, learning to let go of control in a situation or finally tackling your fear of heights. Whatever it is, leaving your comfort zone and learning to better deal with a situation will allow you to become more well rounded and to tackle future situations a lot more confidently.

If you find you are getting really stuck along the way, don't worry. This can take a lot of practice as well as awareness, if you actively try to improve upon something you may feel even more conscious but try making some notes or giving yourself pointers on ways that you can improve.

What do I mean by pointers? So, let's imagine you suck at appearing on camera or a recording, the first step is acknowledging that you suck, the second is trying to figure out ways to not suck. With me so far? Perhaps you say "Uhmm" or "Errr" a lot as a sign of nervousness or room to think. Instead of this, try gathering your thoughts before you speak. Immediately you sound ten times more exciting to listen to. An alternative method is to end sentences and words needing to take a breath, that way you will need to breathe which allows for a natural pause to occur.

Something as simple as taking extra time to gather your thoughts may dramatically help you to improve speaking on video, and maybe help you to feel a little less self-conscious in the process.

Try applying the same concept to your selected "weakness" or "area for improvement". Being able to accept that you don't start off as an expert at anything is really vital – we are often impatient and want to be great at everything we try. After all, when we are good at something we get a sense of achievement and accomplishment by doing that thing.

Just remember that if you practice something enough you are likely going to get better at it, the more you do something the better you will be at it. So long as you have some guidance on how to improve, trial and error does work. If you can take pointers from someone that has already made all of the mistakes, you will learn from not just your own, but theirs' too.

This is one reason I love learning with a group of people or at least a friend, if you are all learning together you will pick up on each others' mistakes. Effectively doubling or even tripling the rate at which you can learn from mistakes! By using the group-learning approach you can often learn much faster.

Becoming self-aware is an often slow process; however, once you manage to achieve it fully, you will have a much better chance of overcoming your weaknesses. Your flaws and quirks will become more apparent to you, as well as how you respond to situations.

Remember, you are only able to control your own response. Not how others respond.

The comfort zone does have its place, though. It is a place where we can reflect and think about the things we have been learning. Without taking time to deliberate in a safe space, learning can become stressful and more challenging than necessary.

Chapter 11

Happiness As A Currency

So here you are probably thinking, "Okay Tali. So what the hell do you mean when you say happiness is a currency?" That's a pretty fair question and one I hope to shed some light upon.

The topic of happiness as a currency has already been brought up, but what does that even mean?

How can an emotion be compared to a currency? A better question I think to ask yourself is, "What is the emotional and physical exchange rate of happiness to you?" That is to say, what are you willing to change to prioritise your own happiness and wellbeing?

Many of us perceive time as a currency and you have to choose wisely how you spend it as it is finite and if we are lucky we get around 4,000 weeks of it, but surely happiness is just an emotion, right?

Much like money and time, emotions are a limited resource, created and spent in a similar fashion. We have a limited capacity as humans, only so many things we can care about before emotional bankruptcy occurs. Once this happens for a prolonged period of time, stress and poor mental health can occur as a result.

For now, let's focus on creating positive moments, or a happier life for us to live. If you want to feel happier then you have to make sure the surrounding people and situations make you feel this way. If work makes you feel fucking awful and you hate your colleagues then that is a big part of your day, you are likely to feel unhappy about this aspect of your life.

I would like to take a moment to highlight that the absence of unhappiness is not the same as happiness. Thriving and flourishing has a lot more to it than simply not being unhappy, just because you are not unhappy does not mean you are doing well and feeling fulfilled.

If happiness is what we want to have more of in our life, then unhappiness is what we are trying to create less of. You will not always be happy but you can have other positive emotions and feelings such as feeling grateful, content and fulfilled.

The first step is to reduce the amount of unhappiness you are feeling, the amount of negative emotions and the amount of time that you are feeling shit about things. If you are unfulfilled and feeling these emotions then something is wrong, this is an emotional response from your body to say something isn't quite right here; something needs to change and doesn't sit right with you.

As you're probably aware happiness comes and goes, it's not generally a constant unless you're genuinely "living your best life" or have some sort of hormone imbalance creating a constant state of euphoria. To be genuinely happy you have to start building a life around you that you are, well, genuinely happy with.

It's not one component of it, it's all of it. Your whole life; work, family, friends, partner, hobbies, spare time and how fulfilling your life is as a whole. Every aspect of your life will contribute to this, but first try looking at the most obvious one that needs to change first.

If we split your life into 4 main segments: Home, Work, Finances and Social which one stands out as the thing making you unhappy? It is also important to look at what is going well for you to have a sense of gratitude, what in your life makes you happy?

Usually one of these aspects will stand out, the one that needs to change for you to continue growing and to be happier and the one that is a source of happiness. If it does not immediately spring out, have a think. Others usually notice mood changes before you do yourself. Has a particular situation or person been draining you recently? Maybe your friends see you show passion and enthusiasm about a particular area of your life. Could this be a source of happiness and excitement?

Many people sacrifice here, if happiness is a currency, what aspects of your life do you have to spend it on? What is exhausting you? What brings you down? This could be a person that is in your life, or it could be an aspect of it that is not aligned with your beliefs and values. The things that drain you and exhaust you, leaving you feeling empty or numb are likely not positives.

The truth is you probably already know the answer to the questions above, but have you explored why this is the case, have you thought about what needs to change? Taking a look at what is within your ability to solve, and what you need help with is a great step to take. Looking after your wellbeing and happiness is not something you should stop doing.

Spend a little time writing down what you would like to change about your life, the first step of making a change is identifying what you want to change. Next, it's all about that change. So you know what to change, but how to do it? This is the tough part, sometimes a slight change is enough, other times it's a drastic change that is required. Sometimes re-balancing is all that is required; all of the components are there but in the wrong ratios for what is right for you.

Be realistic, you know yourself better than anyone else. Are you better at small changes or larger ones? What's realistically required and what can you cope with right now? Sometimes you know what has to be done, but it's the fear of doing it that is holding you back. The truth is, you have to do it. There isn't anything complicated about what you need to do, but it could be fucking terrifying thinking about what needs to be done.

If thinking about making changes causes your chest to tighten and for you to feel nauseous, then I personally think there is even more reason to make those positive changes. If the changes you are making are reversible then stop messing around and make a decision. Inaction is your worst enemy and by getting so caught up in all the possible choices, instead you won't make any choices and be stuck right where you are now. Is that what you want? To be in the same situation you are in now in five years' time?

These are all questions that only you can answer. Your happiness is different to someone else's, own it. It's your happiness after all. Remember that nobody else can truly make you happy; it is an emotion that is felt internally, but external influences can heavily lean into what makes you feel both happy and unhappy. Gratitude for what you have will often help you to appreciate how lucky and happy you truly are already.

Ultimately, this is about your happiness but the choices you make will also affect other people too; don't be reckless here but instead use it as a means of identifying and tackling the elephant in the room.

Most situations can be resolved or improved, so ignoring the issues in your life is not the answer; unless it is in fact your own perspective that perhaps needs to shift.

After reading a fantastic book by Sarah Knight I realised that I have already managed to delve into the world of not giving a fuck. My fuck-o-meter is limited and this helps me to manage my own happiness much better, by not allowing things that mean nothing to me to get to me; such as other people's opinions on things that ultimately have little or no meaning to me.

This is perhaps a result of the humbling experience I had at age twenty-eight, having spinal surgery, not a particularly fun experience and not something I'd recommend to anyone that can avoid it. What it did teach me is that I'm lucky, lucky for all sorts of reasons, but it made me appreciate the use of my legs. After surgery I was worse off than I had been before I went under the knife, unable to sit down for more than a few minutes, in constant pain, difficulty sleeping and walking like an old man was a very humbling experience to say the least.

After surgery I had six week of walking like this, very slow, unable to lift anything heavy, having to roll out of bed and quite honestly struggling to function. The experience has made me thankful for being able to go to the gym, being able to walk, having a now somewhat normal life. Yeah, I get back pain, can't sit for too long and sleep isn't going to ever be the same again, but I can walk. Until you have something taken away from you, until you lose something as fundamental as walking normally, you don't realise just how lucky you are.

The lack of dropped curbs and poorly thought out pedestrian routes through town became a daily issue for me, not something I ever thought I'd struggle with at a young age. Until you are shuffling your way, one small painful step at a time and have to cross the road at a painfully slow pace you may not appreciate the most basic and simple functions most of us have. This made me greatly appreciate how lucky I am, I'm alive, not paralyzed, and can have a mostly normal life.

Until this time I'm not sure I really thought about how lucky I actually am. If anything, I was less fortunate than most others, twenty eight needing to have a spinal decompression sucks. The thing that helped me through this was that it was out of my control, nothing I could do changed the simple fact that my life was going to change. Some things are out of our control, and there is no point worrying about something that you can do nothing about; no matter how much it affects you.

We have a limited resource of energy as well as emotions, it's incredibly important you learn to manage the amount of things that matter to you and the things that you just couldn't give a toss about. Other people's opinions are something I do not care about; or at least I want to care less about and I'm actively learning to care less and less each week. The truth is that it's a work in progress, and that's fine. Change takes time and it is part of life, we become a different slightly better version of ourselves as we learn to grow and adapt.

Sure, some of us can become worse versions of ourselves objectively too, but I'd like to think if you are trying to work on yourself or to develop *you* then you're only becoming more self aware of who you really are.

When you stop caring about the things that don't matter, you can really focus on the things that do matter. These are the things that make you happy, the things that fulfil you; your Ikigai, your loves, your interests, all the things that make life worth living for you. Oh how refreshing it is to have more capacity to care about these things, and to feel less unhappy about the things out of your control.

Next up is a sort of rinse and repeat cycle. When you begin to make positive changes in your life for the first time, it becomes more natural to continue making positive changes, again and again and again. You see, we are drawn to familiarity, if you are used to being treated badly and experiencing negative behaviour then despite the fact that this is awful you will feel a sense of safety as you are used to this. When you begin to change environment, behaviour and habits you can create the new familiar, the new safe. Hopefully a better one that is right for you.

Once you have overcome the mental fear of the unknown, it

starts to become a natural instinct. You start to make changes that improve your happiness out of habit, rather than settling for less than you deserve.

Stop doing things that you hate. Self love and care are incredibly important; putting yourself first for once is no crime. If you don't stop to look after number one (you), then how are you going to look after number two, and three and four? Every time we fly we are reminded to fasten our own oxygen masks before helping others; if you don't help yourself first, you can't help anyone else without impacting yourself for the worse.

Another point I also think is really important is how we talk about and to ourselves. Stop calling yourself stupid, stop calling yourself an idiot or useless. Be kind not just to others but to yourself too. It all starts with you.

By changing how you talk to yourself and think about yourself, others will also start to do the same. You absolutely have worth and you are a valuable person, so start treating yourself as such and maybe others will follow suit. Talk to yourself like you would talk to a friend, stop putting yourself down and believe in yourself and your ability. This is really difficult to do, as a large portion of our thoughts are negative thoughts to try and protect us from perceived danger, but in the modern age this leads to a lot of unhappiness.

Each and every one of you reading this book will feel different emotions right now thinking about this. Some of you won't be fazed by making changes at all, others will find it a new experience but not feel too uncomfortable and some of you will be downright terrified.

Whatever you are feeling, it is personal to you. How you perceive the world will play a big part in this. All the power to make change lies with you, so ask yourself the question again. ***What would you change to be happy?***

Like I've said many times, we are all different. My aim is to guide you in the right direction to start having you making happier choices for yourself, but remember I can't make those choices for you.

In the end, it will come down to you to take control of your life and own it. You are responsible for your own happiness, and therefore for your own unhappiness too. If you do not make yourself accountable for this you are blaming instead, rather than accepting that you have the power to change a situation you are unhappy about. Perhaps it is just the courage to make the change you need to find first.

One of the biggest contributing factors to happiness is freedom; freedom to do what you want and enjoy. Being free from financial stresses but also having the flexibility in your life to enjoy the moments and adventures that you are after. When a situation begins to make you feel trapped, that is a warning light; beware as humans do not naturally like to feel caged or restricted.

This ultimately all comes down to your perspective, if you feel as if you are being forced into doing something, even if it is something you may enjoy you could hate every second of it. When you are freely choosing to do something, it will be a much more enjoyable experience for you because you exercised your right to decide **you want to do this**, not **I am being forced to do this.** There is a huge difference.

Feeling like you are in control of your life and the decisions that you make is a huge part of this. Make those impactful choices and start to put yourself first, you deserve it after all.

If you start to view happiness as a currency, how much money would you trade to be happy instead? How much time would you invest into a future where you are in control?

When you start to view your own happiness as a currency, you may find you are a lot richer (or poorer) than you once thought.

The idea of this section has been to really get you thinking about happiness. You could be a millionaire earning top dollar, your average office-goer who works 40 hours a week to make 20-something thousand a year or you could be on the breadline struggling to afford basic necessities.

The truth is the amount of money that you earn does not dictate how happy you are. Often more money means more stress and pressure, more responsibility and less freedom, different problems that you have to face each day.

Obviously there comes a certain point where financial worries can impact your happiness, being stable financially is important and I would not try to argue otherwise. Once you manage to earn a high enough income to be comfortable, money will no longer make you happy.

Once you reach a certain level of income there are other factors that are much more important to your overall happiness on this planet. Heading back to Ikigai, sense of purpose, accomplishment and reason for doing what you do are much more important for longevity of a job or career, than how much money is in your bank at the end of the month.

Try building your life around happiness instead of just money, balance it out. Don't make rash decisions that could cost you financially, instead try to find a happy balance between happiness, time and money.

Life can often be a balancing act but by starting to consider your happiness as a vital part required to achieve this balance, I would consider this a solid first step. When you start to make changes for the better, future changes in turn become much easier.

Pluck up the courage and start making those changes for the better, you owe yourself that much. Make choices that in five years' time you will look back on and be glad that you made, you absolutely have the ability to make those changes.

So much can change in just five years, your life could look completely different if you are intentional about the changes you are making. Make choices that make you happier in life.

Where do you want to be in 5 years' time? What about 25? Many people struggle to answer this question as they have not thought past their next holiday aboard, never mind five or more years into the future and certainly not 25 years or more.

Chapter 12

Putting the Brakes on Expectations

Comparison and expectations can take away any sense of achievement you may otherwise feel, these days we are constantly bombarded by social media, television and news outlets showing us two extreme ends of the scale. Put the brakes on, and slow it down.

The expectations that we hold ourselves to can work against us if we let our imagination get away from us, if you are aiming to become the one percent of the one percent, you're going to be disappointed. Entitlement is born from this, entitlement that you should be a millionaire, seeing the lavish lifestyle of others, or trying to keep up the illusion that you are living that life. Spending money that you don't have is a trap.

If you start to imagine the perfect life and what you think happiness should look like, you can become so fixated on this that you forget to actually enjoy the here and now; where happiness is really found.

I'm a big believer that we are all in the same storm (life), but we are all on a different boat. Each boat is a different size and can deal with different types of stresses and situations. Start taking a look at your boat compared to those who have a smaller one. It's really easy to look at the largest boats out there and wish for what they had, but this is going to steal you of your happiness.

Comparison is the thief of joy. Your boat isn't gold plated and has the latest engine, so what? Neither does mine! If you are comparing yourself against excellence constantly, you aren't going to measure up. How many people do you know that are super rich, athletic, intelligent, and excel at everything they do? There may be a few out there but honestly, that's in the whole world. You are literally comparing yourself against people who are the top of what they do. The best sports people, the best actors and actresses, the fittest humans, the richest humans, you are comparing yourself against someone who has spent thousands of hours practicing.

Socrates once said "The secret of happiness, you see, is not found in seeking more, but in developing the capacity to enjoy less." Take a moment to reflect upon those words, they have a deep profound meaning.

You are responsible for your own happiness, you are in control of your own frame of reference and how you respond to situations. How you perceive a situation is a choice you have to make, victim mentality can make you deeply unhappy.

Somebody that is selfish and self absorbed will think that everything bad that happens to them is somebody else's fault, never their own. Accountability for your own happiness is important, but so is accountability for your own unhappiness. When you realise you have the power to decide if you are happy or unhappy, you can become unstoppable. The truth is you choose how to measure happiness. You set the expectations, you decide how to measure your happiness, you decide what and who you are comparing and measuring against to determine if you are happy or not. You get to decide if you are measuring against other people, or trying to be better than an older version of yourself.

If you are trying to sell more books than J.K Rowling, earn more money than Jeff Bezos, or be a faster sprinter than Usain Bolt... for the average person like you and I this is never going to be attainable. You're going to be fucking unhappy if you compare yourself against unrealistic expectations, no matter how fast you are or how much money you earn. Your expectations versus reality can massively impact how you are feeling, whenever you compare yourself to somebody that you feel is 'ahead' of you or more 'successful' you are actively robbing yourself of joy. The honest truth is that they probably have their own problems, different to yours but they still have problems, their life is not perfect either. Why expect yours to be?

We all have problems, there is no escape from having problems they are part of life. We do however have different problems, I think life is a little bit of choosing which problems you want to try and deal with each day. A librarian has different problems to a police officer, an acrobat has different problems to a chef. We all have our own things we are dealing with, there is no escaping stress and anybody who tries to tell you otherwise is being dishonest, in my humble opinion. If we become more resilient by dealing with problems and issues outside of our comfort zone, surely having problems isn't necessarily a bad thing?

People can become fixated on what their happiness should look like; this can backfire and have a negative effect on our way of thinking. If your expectations of happiness are too high, you will struggle to truly be happy. Objects and material things aren't going to make you happy, sure they may give you a dopamine hit for a few moments from the excitement, but you will keep chasing this hit again and again. Where does it end? Instead be present, don't take time for granted and make the most of events, time with friends, family and your day-to-day. The things that really matter, the people around you, the events that you go to, your passions in life, that is where happiness is truly found.

I'm not suggesting changes to your life don't need to be made, but mindset and how you perceive the world is incredibly important. Happiness is from within, we are all capable of being happy (certain medical conditions excluded, of course). Planning too far into the future can result in disappointment when expectations are not met, having a realistic approach and acknowledging that you will not *always* be happy and that things will not *always* go your way is equally important.

In order for happiness to really be appreciated, we have to feel other emotions too. There is no emotional-bubble wrap for life; you are going to feel anger, frustration, disappointment, sadness and a wide variety of other emotions too. Taper your expectations, the idea is not to become a being of constant happiness and delight. It is about taking steps to build a happier life for you over time, as well as opening your mind to the concept of gratitude, self-awareness and broadening your horizons.

If you fall into a fantasy where you feel you *should* be happy, you can become complacent or even frustrated because you *want* to be happy but don't feel that way. Action is the most effective tool you have at your disposal. Make sure you keep moving in a positive direction, but be sure to keep grounded and not have your head in the clouds. You will have good days and bad days, and that's OK. We all do, that's normal.

It's a balancing act, but visualising the future you want can leave you so focused on where you *should* be, that you can fall into a vicious cycle of comparison. **Comparison is the thief of joy.** Don't fall into the trap of comparing where you are now to where you think you should be. You are where you are, that is the reality. A tough pill to swallow, but you wouldn't be reading this right now if there was an easy route. There is research to suggest that we overestimate our own ability often, and perceive ourselves as less at risk of bad things happening to us than to others (Kulesza et al., 2023), but this just means we are unrealistically optimistic most of the time when comparing ourselves to the average person.

Social comparison is challenging, it is ingrained in us, something we are not able to easily escape, even if we do not realise we do it. For this reason social media can make us compare ourselves regularly to others and feel bad about it, particularly upward comparison (Nisar et al., 2019; Vogel et al., 2014).

Life is hard; you have to accept it will not always go your way. Try not to fall into the victim mentality, instead make change happen. What is in your control? Is there a different way to look at a situation? How can you change things for the better? Catastrophizing can be a real nightmare to deal with, where you fixate on the worst possible outcome, even when it is unlikely.

When you start to realise you are in control of your reactions to a scenario or a situation, you realise that you also have the power to change things for the better.

Just remember that it's okay not to feel happy too, there are no rules. Don't criticize yourself for not feeling a certain way, this will only make you feel even more unhappy and can be a difficult pit to dig yourself out of.

The negative spiral is a real issue for many, you have a negative thought and then another and then another. By the end of it you're cursing yourself for having a negative thought at all and think you're stupid. Again, this is normal. It's not a good normal but the more you can catch these spirals early, the sooner you can stop them happening. Catch your negative thought patterns before they take hold of you. "Ah shit, I did that thing I said I wouldn't do, I'm such a piece of shit" You're feeling bad for being a piece of shit now, but let's be rational, are you really? No, no you are not. Rational and emotional thoughts both sound the same in your head, don't let the negative emotional responses drag you down.

Take a step back and try thinking about that negative thought you just had, are you being fair to yourself? Are you being rational right now? Take the time to really think about this when you start to have a negative spiral. Talk to yourself like you would talk to a friend, be kinder. Would you say these things to your friend, would you call them a piece of shit?

Happiness doesn't have to be a future goal or state of mind, it can be achieved now. By learning to appreciate the smaller things in life and the current moment you can begin to understand that reaching certain milestones in life aren't what make you happy. Sure, you might feel happy for a period of time but you aren't going to feel that way forever. It's not natural. Focus on being present in life rather than dreaming about a future where you are happy.

Finding purpose and feeling as if your actions are having a positive effect on others and a sense of significance are much more important than the superficial highs from chasing materialistic goals. By feeling valued, useful and that the actions you take are impacting others, a sense of self worth can be found, you don't have to be excellent to impact others in a positive way. Gratitude can also be a brilliant way of appreciating the things that you already have. Now I know, this can sound a bit like hippy shit. If this exercise isn't for you, try travelling. Travel to parts of Asia or Africa where people truly have nothing and you will learn to appreciate what you do have.

Failing a trip abroad, give the below a shot, try writing down things in life that you are grateful for. Try using the below table as a very brief example and guide, here are a few things I am grateful for:

What am I grateful for?	*How does it make me feel?*	*Does everybody have this?*
Having a roof over my head, clean drinking water, heating a safe space to live.	Safe, imagining that some people don't have this is actually quite scary.	Not everyone, most people in the UK but not everyone around the world.
Having food, not having to worry about my next meal.	This definitely makes me feel safe and happy, as a foodie being unable to eat what I want, when I want would impact me deeply.	Again, not everyone has this but a lot of people in the UK don't have to worry about food. But a lot still do.

A job that pays the bills, with a little extra after.	Whilst I may not have the highest paying job, the role itself is something I enjoy. I'm grateful for being able to pay my bills without too much financial stress.	Not everybody has a job, in the UK or around the world.
My family.	I'm incredibly lucky to have a supportive family, I know a lot of people don't have this so I acknowledge I am very lucky to have them.	Some people don't have this, I am lucky in that respect.
Free healthcare.	Until you live outside of the UK this is something you take for granted, Breaking Bad wouldn't have become a series if it was based in the UK. Walter would just have been treated with chemo, the end.	Most people do not have access to free healthcare around the world, in the UK we are lucky.
That I am able to walk, run and enjoy life as normally as possible.	Undergoing surgery was humbling to say the least. I'm grateful everyday that I can go to the gym, go for a walk and even go for short runs that aren't high impact.	Not everyone has this luxury, I realised that after having surgery I am incredibly lucky to be able to walk, run and exercise.

I feel we get so caught up in our own lives and problems that we forget to acknowledge the aspects of our life that we are lucky for. The more you practice gratitude, the more you will realise not everything is as bad as it seems. I do truly hope there are positives in your life; try to take a moment to appreciate some of them. This doesn't mean you have the perfect "dream" life, it means you acknowledge that you are lucky in certain aspects of it.

Gratitude is incredibly powerful; if you ever visit countries that are poverty stricken you will immediately understand how lucky you are to be born in a Western country, with access to so many services that we all take for granted.

Social media can rob us of being grateful for what we have and instead focus on what we don't have. Someone is always going to have a bigger and better boat, be thankful your boat isn't sinking like some of the others out there.

Instead, learn to compare you to yourself. Be a better version of yourself than you were yesterday, last week or last year. You get to decide the metric you are using to measure this, rather than setting materialistic or 'goal' based metrics that you can achieve, try to measure by something you could spend your whole life pursuing, something that you get a little better at each time but can never truly reach. For every goal that you reach you will need a new one to continue chasing, if you decide to compare against something that is personal to you but is vast enough that you can never quite reach it, such as... "To be more honest with people, without being an arsehole", "To create music that I can be proud of", "To make healthier life choices" these are all vague enough you get to decide exactly how you are measuring. If you set materialistic goals like a 5-bedroom house or your dream car, you could be left feeling very empty when you do finally achieve that goal you always had. It may not be all you thought it was cracked up to be; don't let materialistic goals have you feeling empty inside.

Money doesn't bring happiness, it just brings different sorts of problems. Goals don't bring happiness either; they just bring the need for more goals to continue chasing. Try setting out on a self improvement journey with a purpose, rather than an empty idea fuelled by the desire for objects, recognition or fame.

Chapter 13

Side-Hustling Your way Forward

If you are struggling with your sense of belonging, your self-esteem or to earn an income, then this section may be worth considering. Whilst less orientated towards happiness, from Maslow's hierarchy of needs we know that money is still important, at least up to a certain point. Beyond this, a sense of belonging, achievement and self-esteem are things that as humans we crave. If you have been considering a change in career, have been looking to diversify your income possibilities, or perhaps want to gain a sense of achievement by having a business, then read on.

Nowadays a lot of younger people have a side-hustle going. It could be a hobby that blossomed into something more or it was set up with the intention of making money from the get-go. But the fact remains; the modern young adult is trying something new when it comes to business and developing multiple income streams.

This is especially true during times of financial uncertainty, having a back-up or second income can be incredibly valuable. Even if it is a small safety net, this can be built up into a much bigger source in the future. Heck, some people just want to pursue that hobby they really enjoy and they find out it makes a little money on the side. And guess what? Hobbies have no age restriction on them. You can start a new business at 60 or 70, there is no age limit.

The days of a one-page CV are over and it with the internet being incredibly easy to access and social media being perfect for drawing attention to a business, or a side business, now is the best time to really start building.

If you haven't already considered starting a side gig to earn a little extra money, now is the time to look into it. With 2020 being the year of lock-downs and a world-wide pandemic people have had a lot more time to think about what they really want to do and many have had extra time to start acting on it too. The amount of businesses that sprung up out of the pandemic has been huge, but so has the number of businesses closing. As we head into 2025 and finances tighten for many of us, a side gig doesn't sound so bad to me.

With businesses struggling, redundancies being made and even businesses closing down it may seem like a bad time to try and start a new one. Wrong. It is the perfect opportunity to expand an idea you have had into a real business or project. With so many businesses closing, the opportunity for E-commerce infinitely blooms, think of all the possibilities that you can grab hold of.

The numbers of gaps in the market has increased, with viable businesses flourishing and sectors that were already struggling likely to close completely. This creates opportunity for you to fill a certain niche or gap in the market.

As the level of uncertainty over what the future holds being even higher than usual, ensure you are being practical about your idea. Is it a pipe dream or a potential business venture? If the risk is low, I would always advise giving it a try. You learn a lot more from action and failure than you do from deliberating tirelessly.

If you are still unsure exactly what you want to do with your life (like so many of us), then this is also a perfect opportunity to try something you have been thinking of starting up. The best advice that I can give to you is give it a shot; it's much better to regret your action than your inaction in life. At least you can say you gave it a shot, instead of that you regret you never tried when you are older.

Now, like I've mentioned you have to be realistic. But once you have something you feel passionate or excited about, it's time to start planning. Come up with the concept and then research, the internet is right at your fingertips. Explore how viable the idea is and what is required to get you going, once you have reached this stage you are likely to mention it to a friend or family member.

Don't always expect them to support you.

Friends and family often mean well, but they ultimately are not you. If you believe in something and have the drive to get it going, you cannot be put off by negativity. Remember to listen to feedback, but just because one person doesn't like your idea does not mean it is destined to fail.

If you take a look at Dragon's Den, how many businesses have failed to secure investment and gone on to operate successfully? This shows that even professionals in the area can get it wrong, so don't expect your friends and family to know everything, take their opinions with a grain of salt.

Like I said, the best way to do it is to just do it. Learn from mistakes don't end up in the endless cycle of perfection. It is much better to release something that is bad than to release nothing at all. If you are a perfectionist you may never be happy, but perfection is incredibly subjective. Start now, improve later.

The beginning is always the most difficult part, taking a leap of faith is often not an easy step for most, especially if friends or family members are still pecking at your head and not providing any motivational support. You are going to have to learn to self-motivate and drive yourself. Other people will often mean well, but will put you down. Find the courage to stick to your decisions that you truly believe in. You will not always get it right, but without trying you will not learn.

Humans are happy when they have freedom and control; often people do not have control over situations and this can cause unhappiness. This is often seen in work, the constraints of a 9-5, 8-9 or working 12 hour shifts can leave us drained and unfulfilled. Many people during the COVID 19 pandemic took the opportunity that furlough presented them; pursuing their dream job.

Many people decided to use working at home, the government furlough scheme and extra time on their hands to start up a side business, with some even quitting their fulltime jobs entirely to pursue their newfound start-up. The side-hustle isn't for everybody, but it is certainly an avenue worth exploring at least once in life.

There is much to learn about yourself through starting up and creating your own business or side-hustle. You may discover you love accounting, or you absolutely loathe it and would much rather create the product or offer the service, you may even find that you love marketing and social media. This is as much about figuring out what aspects of the business that you excel at and enjoy as creating a successful venture that can turn profit.

One point I will make is that going it alone is a lot harder than being in a team, having worked in both a team and as an individual starting businesses up, I can without a shadow of a doubt say motivationally working within a team was amazing. Of course this can create other issues such as the team dynamic and who takes on what responsibilities but overall motivation levels are a lot higher as you can bounce ideas off one another.

On the flip side, going it alone means you have complete control. You are the business. You are the one that creates a product or service, market it, network with others, ensure that social media is kept on top of, create systems, manage the accounts, the list really does go on. Of course once you manage to scale to a level where you can afford help, you know you are on to a winner.

I do think it's important to remember that just because you **can** do something on your own, doesn't always mean that you shouldn't ask for help where possible. Sometimes friends or family will even help out without payment, usually if you have helped them in the past you can cash in on favours. Likewise, you can always repay friends or family later on when they need a leg-up. If you would rather not ask friends or family, there are plenty of people around the world who are willing to help for the right money. I believe in starting off smaller and scaling, keep things cheap if they don't need to be expensive.

While it may sound like a lot, if you are truly passionate about getting a side hustle or even a business started you should take the leap. If you are unhappy in your current job or feel like it is not right for you, sometimes a change of pace can be the best remedy.

I won't begin trying to paint the picture as an easy one, but the rewards from creating something that is your own and the accomplishment of making it a reality is no small feat. Turning an idea or a dream into reality is an amazing feeling; the whole process is exciting from start to finish.

There are of course hurdles to overcome and costs to foot; as I mentioned, it's a difficult route. The reality is if you want to come into a substantial amount of money then going it alone and taking the leap has one of the highest income potentials, if you have a solid business idea.

Creating a business plan and at least a rough structure of how everything will work is an essential, if you are serious about making it work then I suggest that you get down and dirty with the work. Things will need doing and you will have to be the one to get them done, it's not for the faint hearted or those that lack drive.

Once you have identified a gap in the market and have conducted a little research of your own it's time to make the dream a reality.

Here are a few tips that I would give anybody looking to start their first solo gig or business:

- Be realistic, but also optimistic about your venture. You will have to work hard to bring life to this, who said it would be easy? First, sit down and get the nitty-gritty done. How will the business work? What will it cost you? What will you charge? Can you do all of the roles yourself? How will you source materials or equipment? Do you require suppliers? You don't have to have ***everything*** figured out, but you do have to have a plan to move forwards.

- Create a business plan (even in a rough form), the products or service you are offering, how you will scale, projected costs and charges, your prices, margins, suppliers etc.

- Figure out the investment or costs required, try to keep these low, especially if this is your first venture. Insurances and overheads can quite rapidly sneak up on you.

- Enlist help from those talented individuals that you know. Be sure to call in those favours that you are owed; getting help from family or friends can be an invaluable resource. Don't be too selfish here, though. Make sure you return those favours too!

- Network early, network often. You can learn a great deal from others that have already done what you are looking to do. Networking is vital to build a bridge into the industry, if you already have connections here, even better! Getting your foot in the door is often the hardest part. Starting is never easy, but once you have started and you gain traction it will become much easier over time as you learn and improve.

- Once you have a product or service, come up with a name. I suggest not picking something that is too close to an existing business as your SEO (Search Engine Optimization) will greatly suffer. If you are creating a new business it helps to get listed on Google so people can find you.

- You can check existing business names on Companies House in the UK. If you intend to operate as a sole trader this can still be important, but if you come up with an amazing name you may wish to consider copyrighting as your name will not be protected.

- Once you are all set up as a Sole Trader or Business, it's go time. Get yourself out there, network and spread the word. Depending upon the service or product contacting the local newspaper can be a good way to get your name out there. Papers love to promote, especially local businesses or projects in the community.

- Use social media. I cannot stress this enough, but the likes of Instagram & Facebook are almost an essential nowadays for a new business. When used properly you can go from a regular business to a booming business, just remember to keep the social media updated often. Try not to over think it too much. If you curate your content too much it may feel artificial.

These are just some basic steps to take, there will be a lot more to consider but try not to consider and prepare too much. Keeping it simple is best, you can worry about the fine details later on.

Now I realise that this is not for everybody, there is nothing wrong with having a career and being content in following the progression ladder if it is something that you enjoy and it gives you a sense of purpose. Consider it as a potential avenue to consider, rather than a hard must or must not. Not everybody wants to start their own business or have a side hustle, but I think it's a great thing to explore if you are unsure what job you want to do in life, but have a business idea that has potential. If you are set on having a business and following your Ikigai by means of self-employment or a business start up, then the above is important to consider.

Chapter 14

Surrounding Yourself with Like-Minded People

This section will talk about the benefits of surrounding yourself with like-minded people. This could be an individual or a group of people that think like you or that you look up to and would like to learn from.

Association is important, by surrounding yourself with people who exhibit certain qualities or have knowledge that is important to you (and they are willing to share), you can begin to learn to develop some of those habits or qualities that they possess. This could be as simple as a positive mindset, improving your motivation, or even adopting a certain habit or routine. This is true in all aspects of life, fitness, diet, business, work, mindset, as well as happiness.

You are sculpted by those around you, as well as who you are. If you hang around with a bad crowd for long enough, the behaviour is normalised and you are likely to end up being influenced yourself. The opposite also applies, if you are surrounded by a positive and motivated group of friends or people, the likelihood of you adopting their qualities and values is much higher.

Like I said, you can apply this to all walks of life. If you are trying to become happier, perhaps you need to start looking to hang out with more motivated and happier people. This may allow for you to understand them better, and what they do or how they think in order to be the way they are.

This does not only apply to your mindset and how you think. In business, having a mentor or others in a similar position to you is incredibly powerful. This can help not only gain insight and experience but to help motivate, cultivate and also widen your mind's point of view. Sometimes it does not have to be a mentor or a group of friends, peers are also incredibly useful. If you are not currently in training or education in the specific area you're interested in, try either joining a like-minded community or finding a group of people who share a similar goal to you.

If networking is not one of your strong points, then thank god for the internet. With the internet now literally at your fingertips, you can easily find groups on Facebook or forums that relate to people you either aspire to be like or those that share the same interests as you. Both fantastic tools to help navigate an area you may just be dipping your feet into.

The motivation from this can not only help you to gain insight and tips from others but allows for you to relate back to your own experiences and views. This in turn can really help to benefit your overall drive and give you an instant-leg up in terms of not only your knowledge but your chance of succeeding too.

Here's a good example, whilst writing this book I've begun to join writing and poetry groups on Facebook. This has been perfect to understand other's experiences in the area and also to try and learn more about being an author. Of course I could simply pop to almost any blog post on the topic to try and learn more, but by engaging with others who are in a similar situation, or better yet are on their fifth novel, it allows for me to gain some much needed insight.

You can apply this to pretty much any interest, hobby or goal. Let's say you want to try and improve your fitness, by surrounding yourself with others who are actively trying to:

- Improve their overall fitness levels
- Improve their diet

- Or both

Think about this...

You are going to not only be pushed motivationally by others trying their best but also kick yourself up a notch and perhaps go on to inspire others in the future too. Do you think you are more likely to continue sticking to positive behaviour if you surround yourself with others who do the same, or people who put you down for making a change?

The reason that many friends drift away is that people grow and change, this is natural and people can become so different and opposite that people would hardly recognize them from their younger selves.

This is probably most obvious with childhood friends or school friends after heading to university and coming back, or moving away and then visiting your home town after a few years.

There are many benefits to surrounding yourself with the right sort of people, you are after all a product of your environment but there comes a point in life where you are the one that gets to decide what that environment is.

How can a plant grow without sunlight, nutrients and water? A change of environment or changes to your life can be paramount to enabling you to grow. Sometimes it is the people that you surround yourself that can enable for this to happen. Positive external reinforcement from others can be a blessing, consider the people that are in your circle. Are they the right people that align with you as a person and where you are trying to go?

Taking those with addiction as an extreme example, going to rehab works wonders whilst the person is there. But when people are reintroduced into the same environment, and they get clean an extremely high proportion of the time they relapse. Now, why does a relapse happen? You have just put the person back in the same situation they were in before, the same friends, the same area, and the same access to substances. By changing your environment (geographical or otherwise) you will then see a change in behaviour. If there were no substances to take, how would you become addicted? One of my friends underwent such therapy and due to relocation is now thriving, which is beautiful to see.

I know that is a fairly extreme example, but the same can be said for almost any addiction or negative habit. If you can change your friendship group, change your location, change your job, or change your perspective enough that certain behaviour is no longer normalised, change can start to occur. If you start meeting with a group of people who share a common interest, it will help to reinforce the habits and behaviours of those people relating to that hobby or hustle.

By ensuring that you are surrounded by the right type of people for you, you can begin to see benefits in your creativity, your motivation, adopting positive habits, new routines and improvements to technical skills. Check out local groups in your area, if there aren't any then you have the option of finding an online community that shares your interests. It has never been easier to find likeminded people and connect with them than now.

Chapter 15

Kill Your Ego

The ancient Greek and Romans formed a line of thinking called Stoicism, with many such as Zeno of Citium, Socrates, Marcus Aurelius and Epictetus being known as some of the great philosophers of their time. Epictetus is perhaps one of my favourites due to his upbringing in slavery, despite which he won his freedom and later become a philosopher of Stoicism. Something about the underdog mentality has always fascinated me; perhaps this is why he stands out to me.

The line of thinking of a Stoic is relatively simple; you can control what you can control, and that which is out of your control you cannot. Epictetus once said "There is only one way to happiness and that is to cease worrying about things which are beyond the power of our will." it seems like the Stoic philosophers of their time had figured out one of the elements of happiness. Yet why do we forget something so simple?

Ego is the enemy, "It is impossible to begin to learn that which one thinks one already knows", meaning when we think we have all the answers and have all the information we can become ignorant. Why continue to learn when we already know everything? Or think we know everything.

I learned this the hard way; I learned I didn't know everything. I learned that what I thought I knew about myself and my values could have their foundations shaken to the very core.

Some people might find this chapter quite heavy, you've been warned.

Several years ago I was engaged to who I thought was the love of my life, she certainly was at the time and there was no doubt about this in my mind, I don't think there was for the majority of the relationship in her mind either. Looking back our situation was far from perfect and there were perhaps too many hurdles to realistically make it work, one of which was me.

You see, it was a long distance relationship. It didn't start that way but one injustice lead to another and her and her family had to return to the Philippines; a story in itself. I flew over to visit a couple of times, which was a fantastic experience but it was bitter-sweet having to leave to come back to the UK each time.

You see, I had been depressed. Deeply, deeply depressed and struggling with my own mental health and the fact I had my partner torn away from me and flown half way around the globe certainly did not help. To be honest I had been struggling with my mental health before this, but the trips out to see her just made it all the more obvious. It wasn't until the first trip to the Philippines I realised something wasn't feeling right with me, when moments that should be some of the happiest had me feeling shitty and empty inside.

After crying on the beach to my partner one night and speaking to her about my concerns for my mental health. I asked her "Do you think I need to speak to someone?" a question to which I already knew the answer, I plucked up the courage to see a GP when I got back to the UK.

Seeing a doctor was one of the scariest mental health experiences to date, because this was me having to admit that not only was there something wrong with me but that I was going to have to talk to someone about it and confront it head on. Up until now I had decided to hide or ignore these facts, facing them and bringing them to the surface was the last thing I wanted to willingly do.

From the day I booked the appointment until the appointment happening I was filled with dread, two weeks of chest wrenching nausea and panic. I almost cancelled the appointment so many times but finally, the day of the appointment arrived and I had managed to not cancel it.

I remember the consultation well; the doctor in his late 40s or early 50s asking "why are you here today?" I told him it was to do with my poor mental health. He asked me a series of tick box questions to which I provided answers for, one of the last questions stood out in particular when the doctor chuckled then asked me if I had considered killing myself or not. I paused for a moment, and then answered the question honestly, "Yes" I said. His chuckle cut short as he realised I really was quite serious and not joking about feeling suicidal. After some assurance I wasn't going to kill myself, the consultation ended and I was referred onto cognitive behavioural therapy, the waiting list for which was around nine months. A period of time I thought most people would die waiting for their first session, as they struggled with their own mental battles.

I don't think I realised to begin with how bad I was, there had been signs but it wasn't until the obvious ones such as mood swings, and outbursts hit that I started to hate myself and how I acted. Everything I thought I knew about myself was thrown out the window to be replaced by every negative emotion you can imagine. I don't tell this story for pity; I tell it because this was perhaps the biggest catalyst for me to begin working on myself. But that doesn't come just yet; there was a single moment that everything changed for me in the months to come.

After coming back from Asia for the second time, I was putting more and more pressure on myself to make the relationship work. Newly engaged and wanting to meet the financial requirements to bring her back over to the UK, this had me working jobs I hated to try and make as much money as possible to meet the VISA and marriage requirements the government set out for those would-be long distance couples. On top of trying to make a relationship work, we were separated by an 8-hour time difference that was starting to take its toll on me. Spending time staying up late or waking up early to try and catch a call or message was challenging at best.

I woke up one day after a night out, drinking had become a regular occurrence for me then and I seemed to be out most weekends around that time; at this point I'm not sure if alcohol was the cause or the cure. I had a call from my then partner, somewhere between the inconsolable tears and the splutters over the phone I made out what she was saying.

You see, I had cheated. On a drunken night out I made out with another girl, even now the memory is hazy at best. But there is no doubt in my mind that this happened, it was real, not some alcohol-fuelled dream.

10am the following morning when hungover however, this was not so clear to me.

Being a cheater and knowing about it is one thing, but being a cheater and not even being aware until confronted the next morning was the worst. Waking up to the person you supposedly love crying down the phone, demanding to know what happened the night before and if I had kissed another girl was quite another. Somebody that she knew had seen me out in town and had seen the whole thing, for which I am now grateful for. But at the time I obviously was not, the worst part? I couldn't even fucking remember it happening. Drinking until I was blackout drunk, unable to see properly, with huge portions of my night missing was all too regular of an occurrence for me back then.

When you think you know everything about yourself and then realise you don't it can be quite a shock. I thought that no matter how drunk I got I would never cheat, not even consider cheating.

To have your own values challenged by yourself like that is an eye-opening experience. One moment you're the guy who is madly in love, the next you're the bad guy who has hurt the person you love perhaps more than anyone ever has before. To come to terms with this was difficult, for anyone that has ever cheated on someone before that you care about, it is one of the single worst feelings to experience.

You cannot escape it, you cannot escape yourself and the hatred you can have for yourself and your actions. The next four months were some of the most difficult; we stayed together for about that long before she finally broke things off. Despite my best efforts to try and make things right, the trust had been damaged and once the trust is gone there is really nothing left to keep you both together in a long distance relationship.

Having been cheated on before when younger I knew what it could feel like, I hated cheaters and to become the very thing that you hate was perhaps the hardest. *I was a cheater.* Nothing changed that, *I had hurt the girl I loved.* Nothing could change this either.

Eventually I worked through this, it took a long time to question who I was and to figure out my needs and wants from a relationship. Physical touch and intimacy were obviously much more important than I had realised. The combination of alcohol and depression had brought this to the surface, I think perhaps looking back I was unhappy in the relationship and what it lacked I had tried to find outside of it.

When I think back on this experience now, some part of me is glad that I was seen kissing that other girl. Not because I wanted to hurt my partner, not because I am proud or glad about the act of cheating. Simply for the reason that this experience is the most character changing experience I have gone through in my life so far. Part of me wonders if this hadn't happened would the depression have won? Would the relationship have broken off anyway just due to the strain that was already on the two of us?

When you challenge who you are, who you think you are and who you really are and break them down to the very core, you learn something about yourself. I spent endless nights questioning who I was, I had never imagined I was capable of cheating. It wasn't something I had ever done before and it wasn't something I thought I could do. But I did, it had happened. The four months before the breakup were terrible, with me trying to prove my love and her doubting it constantly. You can hardly blame her; she knew too many who had been cheated on and vowed to never let it happen to her and to tolerate it. These were her values, and you had to admire and respect them. They were honest and pure.

My ego and values on the other hand had been challenged by this experience, having to accept I was capable of betraying trust when I had been so sure I was not capable of this was a tough pill to swallow. I thought I knew myself and my values but in order to discover who I really was, I had to unmake myself first.

This started when she finally broke up with me. After the breakup I immediately went on a sexual rampage, sleeping with anyone I could to try and numb the pain. It wasn't until the lust had passed and I had gotten everything out of my system I could truly start to work on myself.

I began to sort my shit out, I started looking after my mental health better than I had been, I went teetotal and started to work on myself properly; to put my needs first and to focus on getting better. What I had not realised was that in the state I had been I was not ready for a serious committed relationship, especially not one that was long distance. There were still deep scars from an emotionally abusive relationship I had been in previously, I suspect part of the reason I cheated was linked to this, but this is not a topic I am ready to discuss in this book and is perhaps better suited for a session with a therapist than for me to write about here.

Thankfully, after a while my mental health started to improve, the weight of trying to bring her back had been bringing me down; the relationship had been straining me more than I realised. After this I spent a long time single, not wanting to take the risk of hurting somebody again by betraying their trust.

The whole experience was a deeply painful one, but for this reason I also think it was perhaps the most transformative as well. When we are dealt a shit hand, or have to deal with our shitty life choices we have two options; wallow or flourish. Deep pain can be used as a motivator to sort your shit out, rock bottom is the best place to build from, and the only way is up.

The building didn't happen overnight; it has taken years to get to where I am today. I am thankful for the bad times, because they do make you appreciate the good ones. After these events I am a different person, more aware, kinder, and more conscious of others and myself. This wasn't an accidental process, I have been very intentional about improving myself and developing who I am, with plenty more room to learn, develop and grow still.

Being able to sit here, look back on events and write this book is a strange experience. Most people don't like to admit their shortcomings, and even fewer would consider writing about them. I suppose I'm one of those few, but without this experience I would not be the person I am today. Whilst I don't claim to be a saint, I have certainly matured and grown since this time of my life. Being able to accept that the younger me had many flaws, my ego getting in the way of being able to accept who I was, the things I was capable of and the hurt I could cause others certainly held me back. Now I just accept that I can be an arsehole, I do have the capacity to be one but day-to-day I try not to be one.

As the wise Epictetus said "If you desire to be good, begin by believing that you are wicked" this experience definitely had me thinking I was wicked. So much so that I wanted to prove it wrong, I wanted to be a good person. I wanted to prove myself wrong, that I was a good person that had made a bad decision, not a bad person that was just being bad.

Accepting you are capable of something and doing that something are different, acknowledging that you are not perfect and have room to grow as a person is required to actually grow as a person. If you don't kill your ego, it could continue to get in your way of growth. We get to define who we are by our actions and our reactions; others get to decide what they think of us and form their own opinions. We are only in control of half of that sentence; we are only in control of ourselves.

I stayed single for 6 long years, until someone really special walked into my life; my current partner. I still have fears surrounding monogamy and if I will ever hurt my partner, but by being open and honest with her this has made it much easier. I have been able to be open about my mental health, which she has been a brilliant with. She is patient, understanding and able to say the right things at the right time. To get to this point, I have worked on myself for those 6 long years, and each day I still try to be a little better than the last. It's not easy and honestly some days are tougher than others, but mental health is not linear and relationships are not always easy.

The take-home message for this chapter is that for me to grow I needed a catalyst for change, for me that was in the form of hurt. When you want something enough you can get it, but your motivation has to be strong, and boy mine was a strong emotional want. Look at yourself and ask the question, why do you want to change? Why would you like to grow? Sometimes proving somebody wrong is enough, sometimes that person is you and sometimes it is another person in your life. When you think you know everything you leave no room to learn, accepting that you don't know everything is an important first step. Be willing to get your hands dirty and do the work, change doesn't come easy after all.

Chapter 16

Growing As a Person

Personal growth is incredibly important during life, professional growth, practical growth or looking inwards to our personality and values.

If we talk about professional development as skills that you use for work, then practical life skills are the skills that we use for, well, life. Which let's be honest, can be pretty broad depending upon what your life entails. Usually these are things such as changing a car tyre, cooking, using a washing machine and any other essential skills in your day-to-day as a human.

Personal growth is what I'd consider as anything that can help you to develop as a human, put simply, being a better version of yourself. This could be developing how you think, how you process and how you react, there are all sorts of ways to do this from educating yourself to learning more positive behaviours or habits, or challenging the way that you think.

This can often be talked about as growing as a person, ranging from social skills to improving your confidence. Earlier on I talked about surrounding yourself with the right type of people, when growing it is incredibly important to do this.

Growth can often be uncertain territory, meaning it can be a little scary and uncomfortable at times. The main piece of advice I would try to give here is to be yourself and care less what others think. Caring less about what others think does not mean you are actively trying to upset them, or do whatever you want with no regard to others. It just means you are less swayed by the opinions of others and what they think about you in life.

Finding the right type of people to help ensure you are in the optimum space to grow is important. Those that put you down have to be ignored or distanced; otherwise you could find it difficult continuing to grow. Everyone is different however, and some may see this as a motivating factor to prove others wrong. If you want to prove somebody wrong so badly that you push yourself forward, again and again until you succeed, I'd say that's a pretty strong motivating factor. Perhaps not the healthiest, but a strong emotion and desire.

Once you are able to let go of the notion that what other people think matters, you can truly start to grow in incredible ways. Listen to your instincts, what feels right to you? Don't let someone else's opinion stop you from doing what you want to do.

If you are passionate or love to do something, then do it. If you are too afraid to do it for fear of judgement or ridicule by others then you will never manage to achieve your goals. Having the self-confidence and composure to not only try new things but enjoy them can be a huge door-opener.

Trying new things creates opportunities; opportunities can lead to developments in life that you never thought possible. When you start to embrace change and opportunity there are an infinite number of directions that your life could take. Opportunities do not create themselves, despite what people may say, you continuously put yourself in a position where opportunity presents itself until it finally pays off. This is repetition, not luck.

By meeting new people, trying new activities or networking with others you can really start to open doors, doors that may have previously been closed as more and more opportunities start to present themselves. Creating more of a "yes" mindset can put you in some fantastic positions that otherwise may have not been available to you. Just don't let others take advantage of this; saying "no" can be just as important at the right times.

As you start to grow more and more you will become a lot more self-aware, at least, that's the idea. By becoming self aware you can start to see how your actions and words impact upon others too; this is important, as humans tend to mess up a lot, it's how we learn.

Don't be afraid of mistakes, own them. This can be really uncomfortable as admitting that you were wrong or made a mistake is never easy. The truth is people will have a lot more respect for you in the long run for being honest. Having the integrity to hold up your hands and admit when you are wrong goes a long way in life and it's something that can really enable you to grow. As humans we need to be allowed to make mistakes to grow and learn. To become 'good' at something you have to fail at it many times to improve, the same is true for mistakes. Treat a mistake as a learning opportunity, so long as you learned from the mistake or behaviour it was not all bad.

In life I've made plenty of mistakes, but each one has helped me learn, enough failures compound into life lessons that can help to guide you in the right direction for you. As you become more self aware you will also change the language that you use, there are certain words I have completely cut out of my vocabulary and moved away from over the recent years.

Some are derogatory words that no longer serve me, some are words that are negative and have no place in my life, others are words I have become educated on not using as they offend others. Words are powerful, what you say and do does directly influence how others feel. It's important to remember that whilst we are trying not to care what others think, that does not make it acceptable to hurt or upset other people; especially intentionally.

Your liberties end where another person's begin. If you are

directly upsetting or hurting other people because you feel entitled to do so, perhaps you need to take a step back and reconsider your actions and words.

A great little technique I have found is taking longer to respond in a situation where two sets of morals or values are clashing against each other. Add in an extra five seconds of thinking time before you respond. Gather your thoughts; be intentional about your words and responses. Use the five seconds to take a deep breath and calm yourself before replying. We often only see from our own perspective, why has the other person reacted the way they did? Are they having a bad day? Is a relative ill? Are they stressed? Maybe their cat got run over? We. Just. Don't. Know.

If you can remain in control of your responses people will respect you an awful lot more. I'm not suggesting that you let people walk all over you, like I said. Liberties end when another person's begin. If someone is directly doing something to make your life difficult or to try and hurt you, it is completely acceptable to stand up for yourself.

Now that the side tangent is over, back onto mistakes.

It's much better to accept that you messed up and move on from it, learn from your mistakes, don't hide them or regret them. This is where the reflection process can come in incredibly handy, how do you continue to improve and better yourself? Each time you fail, you grow a little bit stronger and better prepared than last time.

Try to see each mistake that you make as a step forward rather than a failure. Many people have their confidence knocked when failing, but being able to continuously focus on moving forward will make you an incredibly strong person. Failure is not failure; it is the form in which we learn best. Try seeing it as a learning process by doing, rather than a negative experience. By managing to change your perspective on this you can achieve much more.

Enjoying the process of learning and by that nature failing is important. To become good at something, unless you have a natural talent, you will need to practice. The number "10,000" is loosely thrown around, that is the amount of hours required to put into something to become a master at it. Now, let's be honest for the majority of skills we are not going to spend that much time perfecting it, unless you are really trying to become a master. The principle still holds true, though.

Practice makes better, so go ahead and enjoy the process of learning. By enabling yourself to enjoy something, rather than fearing it, you will naturally begin to shine more as a person.

Very few of us are naturally good at anything until we put the hours in and fail many, many times. We aren't born experts, we have to become them. I train people in my 'normal' job, and you know what? I let people fail; I let them make mistakes so they can learn from them.

Of course, I never allow for mistakes to happen that could put somebody at risk, but thankfully almost all of the mistakes I allow to happen are very low level mistakes that allow for the person who I am teaching to learn, to be given the breathing room to develop themselves. If you have become scared of making mistakes and worrying about what others think, too shy to try something out of fear of being bad at it... Then this message is to you.

For most people growth can be a little uncomfortable, especially when you are first starting to move out of your comfort zone and push your boundaries. Keep at it, eventually growth comes a lot more naturally, approach it with an open mind and accept that you are not the best at it. Give yourself room for failure, to learn. Enjoy the process; the journey is perhaps even more important than the destination.

Chapter 17

Creating for Others

Eventually you will naturally reached a point where you are somebody that people want to be around, look up to and also learn from, now could be the time to start giving back. You may think "But I don't have anything to teach others!" I would argue that many of the great artists and philosophers of their time were nothing but ordinary people who had followed their values and mission in life. Until their deaths many had paid them little attention, success isn't born overnight.

Sometimes what you are striving for can take many years to accomplish, but that makes it all the more worthwhile when you reach your lifelong ambition. The philosopher Aristotle believed this was the case, ***"Happiness is not pleasure, nor is it virtue. It is the exercise of virtue. Happiness cannot be achieved until the end of one's life. Hence it is a goal and not a temporary state."*** whilst certainly an interesting view to take, perhaps not a view I personally share. Many of us provide value already and certainly can teach others something, perhaps you agree that Aristotle has a point, which then becomes a debate between if eudemonia or hedonia are the 'true' meaning of happiness.

To make that a little clearer for some of you, the ancient Greeks had two words they often used to describe happiness. The first being hedonia, referring to happiness through enjoyment or pleasure, this can refer to simpler forms of sensory pleasures such as food, music, sex, events or watching your favourite film. The second, eudaimonia, on the other hand refers to self-growth or self-actualization, it can be described as fulfilment and I view it as somewhat akin to Ikigai and your reason for being.

The fun thing is we get to decide for ourselves what the true meaning of happiness is. I believe that the two are vital to truly be happy and to lead a fulfilling life.

I'm not saying for you to be recognised and to provide value it is going to take your whole life. The chances are that you have a quality or a skill that others would like to learn or possess, is there a way that you can give back? This could be in an individual setting or to a crowd of people that want to learn from you and for you to provide value to. Think about how you'd like to get the information or teaching across, let's talk platforms and methods.

What platform suits you best, video, written, spoken? Maybe it is less a skill that you want to pass on and more a creative piece that expresses you. There are many forms of expression and creative outlets are fantastic to put your own personal flare out there for the world to see.

Think about who you are as a person and what you are passionate about, what would you like to share with the world? What makes you who you are? What would you like to leave behind and be remembered for once you are gone? Your actions can ripple and impact others for many, many years to come, what will you be remembered for? Build something that you can be proud of, something that has a lasting positive impact upon the lives of others for many years to come.

If you have something that you want to share, different platforms may be more suitable to you than others. If you are using a mobile and wish to use video then Instagram can be great, while if you are recording with a camera then Youtube or video format may be more appropriate. With technology and software advancing rapidly, this can all change though.

If you are naturally a writer then written may be the most suitable, blog posts or even books could be for you. It really comes down to what skills you possess and what information you are trying to share. Think about what you are trying to teach, or the point you are trying to get across. If you were going to learn the skill again yourself, what formats would you benefit from the most?

Focusing on this medium first that you are most comfortable with is a great starting point, but also remember that people learn differently from one to another. Try not to tunnel-vision your medium, having two or three can be ideal to help an array of people to learn and absorb your content.

Seminars or group sessions, which can be recorded and used digitally, are also an option. Running a course to teach a limited number of people is a fantastic way to pass on to group of people, especially if it is quite a personal teaching. Nowadays there are a good variety of online courses you can enrol in, or even run yourself. These are often pre-recorded with tests in them, or demonstrations of a particular skill that others may wish to learn.

The benefit of running an online tutorial or course is that others can learn at their own pace, rewind, re-watch and ultimately digest it at a speed that suits them. Whilst often not as intimate as face-to-face or 1-2-1 tutorials, if the person running the course deploys this well it could be very near to that experience.

If you find that you dislike video but enjoy speaking, then podcasts can be a fantastic way to enlighten or teach others. There are a myriad of different ways to pass along not only knowledge but also ways in which others can grow as a person.

Managed to sustain a particular positive habit? Maybe you started practicing yoga or meditation and want to share it with the world, sharing the journey can be just as important to those who are where you were before. Humans are social; we connect and network by our shared interests and experiences.

I would always recommend long-life media or writing, videos and the written word can last for years, meaning you could be teaching people years from the time you created the content. Crazy thought, right?

That's not to say that group or one-to-one teaching is not useful. This can be a much more intimate style of teaching; it really comes down to what skills or information you are trying to pass along. Workshops can be fantastic for teaching a number of people; meaning you can split the cost for people attending, rather than charging a premium to just one person to make it worth your time.

The only thing I would say is, if you can record it and upload to the internet you will reach a much larger group of people than you would usually by marketing in your local area. However, the style of advertising is very different. What medium are you most comfortable in? Hone that, and then look to develop and dive into others.

As you can probably see, I am a big advocate for creating content that is re-usable, without sounding washed out and the same as your other content. Videos and blog posts are perhaps my favourite example of this, but blog posts and podcasts are another fantastic example.

Usually I try to hit two different types of medium; audio and visual, but sometimes written on different platforms is good too. Perhaps you want to create a blog and also a book; this would be a fine example of that, as I often blog about many of the topics within this book.

Whatever format you find works for you, spend some time on it, figure it out, master it and then decide if you want to try exploring different avenues. Most people don't spend enough time doing the thing that works for them, chopping-and-changing before results can be seen.

Be consistent, be intentional and really think about what you are trying to achieve. Starting something is better than not starting at all, but sometimes having a rough idea or plan of what you are trying to achieve is equally powerful. If you go in without a plan and want to dive in, make sure you are reflecting upon what is working and what is not at some point.

Being intentional about what you hope to achieve can help you to get there more efficiently. Plan, execute and reassess, or if you find action is more effective for you, action, reassess, plan and then execute again.

Creating is an incredibly rewarding process, especially when others have been able to learn from something you have created. As well as being a rewarding and creative outlet, it is something that many people earn an income from. If you are particularly good at this, you may find that other people are willing to pay to learn from you.

When you set out, try not to focus on just the money. You are likely to create far better creative content and courses if you are focusing on the end goal of teaching others effectively. Also, it shows when all you care about is money. It's not a good look and will put people off quickly. Don't be that ***'guy'.***

Chapter 18

Closing Thoughts and Continued Practice

These are some of the key things I wanted to cover in this book. Rather than dragging it on unnecessarily go back, try some of the methods and suggestions that have been talked about and see how they work for you. Some may work, some may not. Without trying, none of them will work for you.

Being open minded and willing to change are perhaps the two things that are the most important. Without either of these you will find it difficult to make changes to your life. We often become happy within our comfort zones, but if you are too comfortable you will not be learning and developing as much as you could be.

So long as you are happy, this is okay. Happiness is really the core of all of this; if you are already happy then perhaps you do not want to make changes. However, if you are reading this I expect there is at least one thing in your life you would like to change.

The parting words I will give you is to not be scared, try making changes and see how it goes for you. Mindset and habits can be changed and formed over time, don't change too much at once.

Start small, but make specific changes you are able to measure somehow. When you start to see improvement in a measured sense this can be very motivating.

Happiness as a whole is more difficult to measure; it is an emotion and a sensation. Finding more freedom in your life and you having more control is something you can measure. Compare your good days to your bad days, are you feeling more content each week as a result of the changes you are making? Remember, change can feel difficult at first but once you start making positive changes it gets easier over time.

Happiness is in the present moment, you can work towards a more fulfilling life but if you are deeply unhappy with your current life and circumstances, you have the power to change that. You hold all of the keys to your own happiness, making the choices that shape your life around you.

If the choices you have made previously are not making you happy, perhaps it is time to try new ones instead of repeating the same behaviour, mindset and patterns and expecting a different outcome each time. "The definition of insanity is doing the same thing over and over and expecting a different result". Perhaps it is time to take a new approach to happiness; otherwise you may find the continued pursuit of happiness leads to a long road of unhappiness, pursuing something that is always just out of reach.

Happiness is an intrinsic emotion, not a goal or achievement which causes a fleeting sense of accomplishment, I hope this book has shown you that much. Ground yourself in the present, instead of daydreaming about the future. This is where real happiness and a real sense of contentment can be found. Stop giving so much of yourself to things that don't matter, learn to say no to the bullshit but say yes to things that align with your beliefs and values.

Lastly, I hope you have enjoyed reading this and found some use from it. We are all in different situations and at different points in our life, but remembering to prioritise your wellbeing and happiness is something that should be at the forefront. After all, we all want to be happy. Just remember there is nothing wrong with feeling another emotion, happiness is an emotion and you will not always feel this way. Practice being present, try noticing and appreciating the small things in life that would otherwise pass us by. Don't worry if you don't feel happy, repressing emotions isn't going to make you happy, it'll make you deeply unhappy and nobody is supposed to permanently feel in a state of euphoria. Feel whatever emotion you feel and start to add more things you care about into your life and start taking those things you don't care about away. It's a simple as that in theory, but much more challenging in practice.

You have all of the tools that you need to start creating a happier life for yourself; my hope is that this book has started to get you thinking about the changes that you would like to make in order to begin working towards your version of happiness.

And with that, I hope that you can start to make more choices in life that prioritise your wellbeing and sense of purpose. Remember you are not alone, and are worthy of being happy. You have the power to change your life and the ability to flourish as a human. I wish you all of the best on your journey, wherever it may take you.

References

Abi-Jaoude, E., Naylor, T, K., Pignatiello, A. (2020) Smartphones, social media use and youth mental health. *Canadian Medical Association Journal.* 192(6), 136-141.

Bamalan, O, A., Moore, J, M., Khalili, Y, A. (2023) *Physiology, Serotonin.* Treasure Island (FL) StatPearls Publishing [Internet]. Available from: https://www.ncbi.nlm.nih.gov/books/NBK545168/

Behere, P, B., Kumar, K., Behere, A, P. (2017) Depression: Why to talk? *Indian Journal of Medical Research.* 145(4): 411-413.

Beyari. H. (2023) The Relationship between Social Media nad the Increase in Mental Health Problems. *International Journal of Environmental Research and Public Health.* 20(3) 2383. doi: 10.3390/ijerph20032383

Chiappini, S., Vickers-Smith, R., Guirguis, A., Corkery, J. M., Martinotti, G., Schifano, F. (2022) A Focus on Abuse / Misuse and Withdrawal Issues with Selective Serotonin Reuptake Inbhibitors (SSRIs): Analysis of Both the European EMA and the US FAERS Pharmacovigilance Databases. *Pharmaceuticals.* 15(5), 565. doi: 10.3390/ph15050565

Davies, C., Knuiman, M., Rosenberg, M. (2016) The art of being mentally healthy: a study to quantify the relationship between recreational arts engagement and mental well-being in the general population. *BMC Public Health.* 16:15. https://doi.org/10.1186/s12889-015-2672-7

Florea, T., Palimariciuc, M., Cristofor, A. C., Dobrin, I., Chirita, R., Birsan, M., Dobrin, R. P., Padurariu, M. (2022) Oxytocin: Narrative Expert Review of Current Perspectives on the Relationship with Other Neurotransmitters and the Impact on the Main Psychiatric Disorders. *Medicina.* 58(7): 923.

Franko, R., Reyes-Resina, I., Navarro, G. (2021) Dopamine in Health and Disease: Much More Than a Neurotramitter. *Biomedicines.* 9(2): 109.

Garcia, H., Miralles, F., Clearly, H. (2018). *Ikigai: the Japanese secret to a long and happy life.* Large print edition. Waterville, Maine. Thorndike Press Large Print.

Gibbs, G. (1988) Learning By Doing: *A guide to teaching and learning methods.* Further Education Unit, Oxford Brookes University, Oxford.

Ginsburg, K. R. (2016) *Building Resilience in Children and Teens: Giving Kids Roots and Wings. [2nd Edition]* American Academy of Pediatrics. Illinois, US. ISBN: 978-1-58110-551-3.

Henderson, C., Evans-Lacko, S., Thornicroft, G. (2013) Mental Illness Stigma, Help Seeking, and Public Health Programs. *American Public Health Association.* 103(5): 777-780.

Ito, E., Shima, R., Yoshioka, T. (2019) A novel role of oxytocin: Oxytocin-induced well-being in humans. *Biophys Physicobiol.* 16: 132-139.

Karim, F., Oyewande, A. A., Abdalla, L, F., Ehsanullah, R. C. Khan, S. (2020) Social Media Use and Its Connection to Mental Health: A Systematic Review. *Cureus.* 12(6) e8627. doi: 10.7759/cureus.8627. PMID: 32685296; PMCID: PMC7364393.

Kiknadze, N. C., Leary, M. R. (2021) Comfort zone orientation: Individual differences in the motivation to move beyond one's comfort zone. *Personality and Individual Differences.* Vol 181. https://doi.org/10.1016/j.paid.2021.111024

Kudrna, L., Kushlev, K. (2022) Money Does Not Always Buy Happiness, but Are Richer People Less Happy in Their Daily Lives? It Depends on How You Analyze Income. *Frontiers in Psychology.* 13: 993137. doi: 10.3389/fpsyg.2022.883137.

PMID: 35719460; PMCID: PMC9199446.

Kulesza, W., Dolinkski, D., Suitner, C., Genschow, O., Muniak, P., Izydorczak, K., Casara, B. G. S. (2023) It Matters to Whom You Compare Yourself: The Case of Unrealistic Optimism and Gender-Specific Comparisons. *American Journal of Men's Health.* Vol 17 (1) https://doi.org/10.1177/15579883231152154

Maslow, A. H. (1954) *Motivation and personality.* New York, Harper & Row Publishers.

Naylor, C., Bell, A., Baird, B., Heller, A., Gilburt, H. (2020) Mental health and primary care networks. *The King's Fund. Centre for Mental Health.* 1-32.

Nisar, T. M., Prabhakar, G., Ilavarasan, P. V., Baabdullah, A. M. (2019) Facebook usage and mental health: An empirical study of role of non-directional social comparison in the UK. *International Journal of Information Management.* Vol 48, 53-62.

Okuzono, S, S., Shiba, K., Kim, S, E., Shirai, K., Kondo, N., Fujiwara, T., Kondo, K., Lomas, T., Trudel-Fitzgerald, C., Kawachi, I., VanderWeele, J. T. (2022) Ikigai and subsequent health and wellbeing among Japanese older adults: Longitudinal outcome-wide analysis. *The Lancet Regional Health – Western Pacific.* (21) 100391.

Purba, K A., Henery, M. P., Henderson, M. Kitikreddi, V. S. (2023) Social media use and the health risk behaviours in young people: systematic review and meta-analysis. *BMJ 383.*

Ressler, J. K. (2010) 'Amygdala Activity, Fear, and Anxiety: Modulation by Stress'. *Biol Psychiatry.* Vol 67, 1117-1119.

Satici, S. A., Tekin, E. G., Deniz, M. E., Satici, B. (2022) Doomscrolling Scale: its Association with Personality Traits, Psychological Distress, Social Media Use, and Wellbeing.

Applied Research in Quality of Life. 18(2) 833-847. doi: 10.1007/s11482-022-10110-7

Seligman, E. P. M. (2011) *Flourish.* Penguin Random House Australia, ISBN 1864712996.

Statista (2023) *Suicide rate in England and Wales from 2000 to 2022, by gender.* https://www.statista.com/statistics/282203/suicide-rate-in-the-united-kingdom-uk-since-2000-by-gender/

Van de Velde, S., Bracke, P., Levecque, K. (2010) Gender differences in depression in 23 European countries. Cross-national variation in the gender gap in depression. *Social science & medicine.* 71(2): 305-313. doi: 10.1016/j.socscimed.2010.03.035

Vaingankar, J A., M van Dam, R., Samari, E., Chang, S., Seow, E., Chua, Y. C., Luo, N., Verma, S., Subramaniam, M. (2022) Social Media-Driven Routes to positive Mental Health Among Youth: Qualitative Enquiry and Concept Mapping Study. *JMIR Pediatrics and Parenting.* 5(1) e32758. doi: 10.2196/32758. PMID: 35254285; PMCID: PMC8933808

Vogel, E. A., Rose, J.P., Roberts, L., R. Eckles, K. (2014) Social comparison, social media, and self-esteem. *American Psychology Association.* 3(4): 206-222.

Zsila, A., Reyes, M E. (2023) Pros & cons: impacts of social media on mental health. *BMC Psychology.* 11, 201. https://doi.org/10.1186/s40359-023-01243-x

Printed in Dunstable, United Kingdom